The Miracle of
CANCER

Dani Gibson

2011 © Dani Gibson
All rights reserved.

Library of Congress Control Number: 2011916799
CreateSpace, North Charleston, SC

ISBN-10: 1466342595
EAN-13: 9781466342590

DEDICATION

This book was inspired and requested by my husband Doni. It was his determination that people could find happiness in life, even while dying.

Doni was my husband, best friend, assistant co-pilot and full time food critic. Doni was also the love of my life and one of God's greatest gifts I've ever received.

I hope that as you read his story, Doni will be an inspiration to you just as he was to me.

Doni,
I have kept all my promises I made to you before you died but to this day the easiest promise was the one I freely volunteered.
" I will love you forever!"
Dani

INTRODUCTION

Cancer is a tragedy for everyone that encounters the reality of it but people live through the story every day and each story is worth telling. Doni was a man of dignity and humor, loving to a fault and never wavered in how he lived...until he was pronounced to be terminally ill. We were given nine months to live a lifetime and each moment was precious and cherished. In telling Doni's story he wanted people to realize that cancer cannot break the human spirit. He wanted people to witness his humor, determination and the truth in living the reality that he was indeed going to die. Doni's story is of being honest within ourselves and with others.

The first few chapters of his book are about finding out that Doni had cancer and about adjusting to the diagnosis. The other chapters are filled with the love and amazement Doni brought to our lives during the last nine months of his life. By the end of the book you will hopefully see the many miracles Doni and I were given through this journey, the main focus that Doni wanted people to see. The miracles were endless!

I pray that I have done justice to Doni's story so that you can see and appreciate life and that your love for God will be renewed.

Although the story is sad it is also filled with countless humor that will hopefully make you laugh and if you laugh just once I will have fulfilled Doni's wish.

Cancer is a powerful word and it can only be dictated by how you accept it and challenge it. The three main stages for cancer are to believe in God, take comfort in each other and love without hesitation.

And the story goes...

"Honey you have cancer, what do you think about that?" Doni is silent for a moment and finally replies "I told you I should have gone to a vet!"

November 28th, 2008

Doni walks into the dining room from the bathroom bent over clutching his chest. His face is gray and he's struggling to get a breath. I grab him and help him sit down at the table.

"Honey, what's wrong?" I ask.

"I can't breathe, I'm going to pass out!" he says.

"Come on we're going to the hospital!" I say near panic.

"We can't go right now" he says, "that lady is coming to get the horse."

"You're kidding right?" I reply to which he says "I can wait!"

2 hours later…

"Honey, are you sure she's coming?" I ask worriedly.

"She'll be here, don't worry" he promises.

Doni's color is better and he's able to breathe a little better. He sees me checking him out and he smiles and reassures me that he's doing okay.

I had called our friend to catch the horse and get it ready so when the woman finally comes the horse is loaded up and taken away with no time wasted. Doni is ready to leave for the hospital and that's the first clue that something is wrong, he's not objecting.

Little did we realize as we leave the house that today was going to be the first day in a new life for us.

Chapter 1

I park the car at the entrance of the hospital ER and run to the receptionist. I tell her that my husband is ill and I need help getting him into the hospital. The receptionist asks for details and I explain that he's having chest pain, having trouble breathing and that he's pretty much unable to walk. I see a wheelchair and leave the receptionist to retrieve it and head for the car. By a miracle I get Doni into the chair without incident and push him back into the ER receptionist's office and he begins answering questions as I go move the car.

When I return they're already prepared to take him back, no waiting this time. We are delivered to a room and the nurse starts asking questions and begins taking his vitals. The attending ER doctor is no time in coming in. He too asks questions, looks at Doni, takes both of our hands in his and tells us he won't leave the hospital until we know what's happening with Doni. He releases our hands and leaves, all Doni and I can do is look at each other with bewilderment. Finally Doni breaks the moment when he begins to laugh and asks "Just where have we landed?" We are both stunned because this doctor is so caring and genuinely concerned. We both feel better already.

The tests begin. The blood work results will be the longest wait we are told. Doni and I are rarely left alone for long and I found it so comforting that I never stopped to think the reason why was because they were concerned he might die. The doctor returns a few hours later with the x-rays and as he puts them up on the board he asks us how we want him to speak to us. Doni tells him to be straightforward and let us deal with the truth.

I take Doni's hand and he squeezes mine reminding me that we're in this together as always, no matter the news. The doctor points to something on the x-ray and tells us that Doni has a massive blood clot between his heart and lungs causing an insufficient oxygen supply to the organs. The doctor continues by telling us that Doni's condition is life threatening and arrangements were being made to life-fight him to Salt Lake City, Utah. The doctor stops for a few minutes to let the news sink in and then continues to tell us that since we have asked him to be honest with us he feels he must tell us that in his opinion Doni won't survive the trip. Boy did that one hit from left field, neither of us had any idea it was going to be this serious. The doctor tells us he has to finish making the arrangements for the trip and leaves the room.

Doni and I sit alone, stunned. Our tears begin to flow as we adjust ourselves to the truth we were just given. I look into Doni's eyes, bend over and kiss him, telling him how much I love him and that I have no regrets for our lives together. Doni smiles at me and tells me in his own words that he feels the same and thanks me for loving him. Silence comes over us again so we hold hands and look at each other like we may never have the opportunity again. Doni breaks the silence by asking me if I'm okay.

My world has just been knocked out from underneath me but I smile and tell him we'll get through this like we always do; together. We sit in silence again as words aren't forthcoming then Doni begins telling stories of our lives together and chooses his most treasured memories. With each story told we again build up our strength and determination and begin preparing ourselves to deal with whatever comes next. Doni has always been my strength and holding his hand I believe I can handle anything. Bonnie & Clyde, George & Gracie, Fred & Wilma, yep that's us!

Chapter 2

Our time alone ends as the members of the life-flight team arrive and begin filling the room with equipment and their personnel. I kiss Doni and tell him I will go outside so they can have more room to work. Stepping outside the room I take my first deep breath. I look down the hall to see our ER doctor talking to someone from the life-flight team. I hear something in their conversation but can't (or won't) distinguish what they've said. The doctor turns my way and I can see my answer on his face, something is wrong.

Getting up my courage I walk toward them and see the same look on the life-fight member's face. The doctor asks me to come into his office so we can talk and I can see the anxiety in his eyes which confirms my belief that I wasn't going to like this conversation. Sitting in his office the doctor takes a few minutes to gather his thoughts and then asks me if I want him to speak frankly with me as before. "I want you to be honest with me" I reply. The doctor sits quietly for another minute then takes my hand and tells me that Doni has cancer and that it has metastasized. I'm in shock and all I've really heard is "terminal" and "do we tell Doni?" The only words I can get out of my mouth are "Excuse me?" and the doctor repeats what he's just told me. There is no hesitation in my decision to tell Doni, he deserves the honesty he's always contained in his life. I get up from the chair and leave the office to go tell the love of my life that our lives have just been shattered, permanently!

What happened? A minute ago we were friends and now our hearts see each other as more. I didn't see an arrow, did you feel one? Our smiles betray a new bond, one to be kept secret for a while. You are still a new widower and people wouldn't understand. Do we fight? How do we do it? Do we fight these feelings we have and pretend they don't exist or do we fight to be together and try to keep it hidden from others? Dani and Doni, is this a sign or what? We don't have to flip a coin; God will decide and tell us, in His time.

How did this happen? We have 15 years difference between us; you have only had one previous relationship, the wife you just lost to cancer. I am from a different age, more liberal with a relationship, which is why you have nicknamed me your little hippie. In spite of the differences we can see the truth of each other's hearts and that is where we want to be for the rest of our lives.

My eyes are going to betray us but that is how I am, real to a fault. We are being surprised with each other. I am finding a wonderful sense of humor in you and my romantic soul is turning you into mush. I sing love songs to you and tears come to your eyes, you are teaching me about the simplicity of life and how to dream. There is a beautiful light in your eyes and I feel amazing strength in your touch. You see the simple heart I possess, and you are finding meaning again to your life since your wife passed away.

I am nothing like your wife but you said you wanted something different. Boy are you getting what you asked for. Good luck honey!

Chapter 3

The doctor is walking behind me as I head towards Doni's room. I see my son and motion for him to come down the hall to us. I introduce Jeremy to the doctor and then tell him the news of Doni's cancer. The doctor explains the details to my son as he just told me and my son remains speechless. I don't wait for a comment. I continue down the hall and enter the room to hear Doni joking with the members of the life-flight team and everyone is laughing. Not wanting to break up the moment or knowing how I am going to handle telling Doni the news, the doctor sees my hesitation and steps in. He asks the life-flight team to give us some time together and they go into the hall. The doctor waits for me to start but I cannot utter a word, I can only take Doni's hand.

The doctor tells Doni about his cancer, that it has spread to other parts of his body and that it is terminal. Tears come to Doni's eyes and my heart rips open with every tear he sheds. I bite my lip to keep from completely falling apart, Doni doesn't need that now. He grips my hand tightly and tells me he loves me and that it'll be okay. Doni never lies to me so I relax, just a little. The doctor leaves the room and the life-flight members come back in and start strapping Doni on the gurney for transport.

The time is gone and I realize that I may never see him again. We take each other's hands and hold on for dear life. I bend down and he kisses me. Is this goodbye? He tells me he'll see me soon and as they begin to wheel him out he squeezes my hand and tells me he loves me. I squeeze his hand back and tell him I love him too. As they exit the hospital I yell to him "Play nice with the kid's honey!"

As my kids were growing up we began having trouble with my daughter. She had no desire to go to school or to have friends and she was constantly challenging authority. She was jealous of her brother Jeremy who was very bright to the point he had been titled "gifted".

Jaime had no idea she was just as bright as her brother so she spent no effort in proving herself, until fate stepped in and she entered a writing contest that she actually won.

The story Jaime had written told that when her dad (Doni) had been a little boy all cats had short tails. The story continued saying that Doni had a pet cat that followed him to school and waited outside for Doni to get out. Going on, Jaime told how one day while the cat was sitting outside the school a dinosaur happened by and accidentally stepped on the poor cat's tail. Of course, the punch line was that as the cat tried to get *away its tail stretched and that's how cats had gotten long tails.*

Doni and I found it hilarious but it also showed that my daughter had finally accepted him as her dad and was comfortable enough to make fun of him, and his age. We found this as an opportunity to help out Jaime's situation at school so we began telling stories of our own.

We began making up stories about the kids in Jaime's class and told her stories about certain traits they possessed. We would make them real enough that she would somewhat fear the truth but challenge the theory enough to go investigate. With just enough persuasion to find out for herself we would send her off to school with the line "Play nice with the other kids because you just never know". After a few weeks we shortened the phrase to "Play nice with the other kids". The stories; and the phrase worked (through elementary school anyway).

Quoting this line now was not only natural but it made the both of us smile. I watched Doni's face as they put him into the ambulance and I wouldn't leave the parking lot till the ambulance was gone. I was afraid that if I moved it would erase my memory of his face, of that beautiful smile. I stand frozen from the reality that I have to make arrangements for a trip I don't want to take.

My son is waiting for me at my house and while I pack he is going to gas up my car and get some money at the ATM for me. I have no clue as to what I'm supposed to pack and can't concentrate because the house is reminding me of all our years together. I keep questioning if Doni will ever step foot in it again. Who knows what is going to happen, how long we'll be gone, what we'll have to get through before we can come home or if they'll even be a "we" when I return. I fight back the tears because I'm certain if they start they will never end. The bags are finally packed; I have prayer with my son and drive off to the biggest question of my life.

My sister Kathi has made arrangements so she can travel with me, I could never drive the three hours alone. As we travel my heart stops every time my cell phone rings. I'm afraid it is the life-flight team telling me he didn't make it and then I berate myself for having so little faith. I've never been in this situation before I remind myself, nor do I care to be here but I am determined to do whatever is necessary because of the love I have for Doni, my husband and best friend.

Chapter 4

Salt Lake City, Utah

Doni is still alive! Thank God he's still here! I arrive outside his room to hear him once again joking with the staff. I enter the room just in time to see blood explode across the room from a vein they're inserting a tube in. Talk about a contradiction, laughter and squirting blood; does it get any better than this? Upon further study of the room I see someone scanning Doni's leg, the pictures displayed on a monitor positioned along his bed.

Here lays the man that stole my heart twenty-one years earlier, the one person I trusted to never break it, but now he has. I know it's not his fault but the pieces are still chipping away, floating off. His smile brings me back to reality. He's obviously enjoying all the attention, LET HIM! I smile back and ask him to tell me what he's found out. He begins by telling me that they'd already told him that the first leg had over 80 blood clots in it. Did I hear right? Dear God, how has he cheated death this long? Sorry God, the answer to that one is so obvious.

The technician inserting the tube finally gets done, the scanning of the second leg is also done and everyone clears out.

I take Doni's hand, kiss him, and tell him how much I love him and how much strength he gives me. My faith in possibility has been renewed but there are so many thoughts running through my mind. Which ones do I verbalize and which do I hide? I look again to his face, at those beautiful shining eyes and I welcome the strength he's pouring through the touch of his hand. I finally find my voice.

"Cancer, honey you have cancer!" The sentence is interrupted as the doctor walks in and tells us that Doni needs immediate surgery to implant a filter to catch the blood clots before they get to his heart or lungs and kill him. There it is again, he may not make it. I have to force the words out of my mind so I can concentrate on what is being said by the doctor. The surgery will take the filter through the jugular vein, a tiny umbrella of sorts, and will implant it around his navel area. This doctor, just as the local ER doctor, states that Doni probably won't make it and so she wants Doni to sign papers stating whether they should resuscitate him or not. We spend a long time discussing and asking questions about each option and the consequences of each. After we exhaust our questions to ask and the doctor has nothing else to address Doni promptly tells her that he wants me to make the decision for him. Shocked by his statement the doctor reprimands Doni and tells him it wasn't fair to think someone else should make the decision.

I know that Doni's scared but I have to stand ground this time and tell him that I won't make the decision but will respect and honor whatever choice he makes. Poor Doni, this whole ordeal must be pure, unbelievable hell for him. How in the world do so many lives get shattered with just one lousy word: CANCER!

Chapter 5

We never get a chance to be alone; the room is constantly filled with nurses, technicians and doctors. All of them going back and forth, their busyness make my head spin out of control and I think I'm actually going to pass out. They announce they're ready to take him to surgery. I'm only allowed time for a kiss, is it the last one? Fighting back my tears I tell him once again to "play nice with the staff". I hear his chuckle as they begin to wheel him out of the room. He releases my hand at the door, I whisper "I'll love you forever" and he's gone. I'd seen the fear in his eyes but I also saw his determination to protect me.

The quietness of the empty room is too much to bear and I break down. Tears fall, unstoppable and I honestly believe I will fill the entire room with them.

I need to make phone calls; to family, work and friends but I don't know how I will ever handle them. "One at a time" God tells me. Calls are made first to my family to update them. Doni is still alive and having emergency surgery to prevent the blood clots from getting to his heart and lungs. Each call I make seems more and more like a horrible dream or maybe a bad television movie. The situation seems unreal, unconnected to us.

Next I make calls to friends to tell them about Doni and I also call work to tell them what's going on and that I'll be gone for God knows how long. Making calls to Doni's family comes last; they don't know anything yet but it has to be done, now. I finally convince myself to just get it over with and the calls begin.

Doni had been widowed for just a few months when we first got together and his family couldn't accept that he wanted to move on with his life instead of mourning for twenty to thirty years. We realized we weren't going to get their blessing even though we were deeply in love. I was prejudged and always felt as an outcast with his family. My first personal encounter with his mom was catastrophic. I was on graveyard shift, Doni on days, when his parents came to visit. They brought their camp trailer and parked it in an empty space next to our mobile home.

One morning I was met with hostility from his mother as she told me their family had never "experienced anything like me". I was torn to shreds for everything from my clothes to my kids. I never spoke back and never went to sleep. Doni came home to find my eyes swollen and he seriously asked "Take up drinking?" I believe my look said everything and he apologized and replied "My mom?" I didn't answer, couldn't even look him in the eyes.

Doni went stomping out the front door and his parents left the next morning. I never asked what transpired and he never volunteered the information.

My first encounter with Doni's kids wasn't any better. They wanted everything that had belonged to their mother and I wasn't to touch any of it because they didn't want my scent on her belongings. Their words and actions were heartbreaking but Doni and I did as they asked. This was obviously going to be the way our lives played out. I was prejudged and I couldn't understand personally how they could do that to me. I decided to be cautious around them but still love them. I was always going to be the outsider, not welcomed but tolerated. Isn't love grand? Good thing Doni was the reward, he was so worth it!

I had no idea what I would tell his family because it was going to hurt no matter what I said. His first wife had died of cancer and now Doni himself was diagnosed with it. I bowed my head and asked God to make my words gentle when I spoke to them. "The truth is what they need" is what comes to me. Okay, here goes.

I make each call repeating the same information over and over. "Yes, Doni is in ICU in critical condition" I would tell them.

"No, the doctors say he may not make it through the surgery but they said he wouldn't make it to Salt Lake either" I continue. I have explained the original diagnosis of the massive blood clot between his heart and lungs, the life flight to Salt Lake and what the emergency surgery is for. Then I give them the news that Doni has cancer and that it's terminal.

They don't realize how badly each word is tearing my heart out. After each call I say another prayer to get me through the next one and also beg God to give Doni and me more time together. "He promised me 40 years" I remind God. I always joked with Doni about how many years we'd been married, how he'd promised me twenty perfect years and twenty not so perfect and was still waiting for the perfect ones to start. Doni had always joked back that he was whipping me into shape and that he was saving the best years for last when I could fully appreciate them. It didn't matter now, I just wanted more time!

The nurse comes in the room and tells me that Doni made it through the surgery and that he was doing well. "Yes God, score one for the home team" I thought. I knew that we'd be thankful for every miracle that came our way and yet being selfish I had to add "And please one more, keep me positive for both our sakes".

Chapter 6

Doni and I had eventually eloped and the judge who performed the ceremony had stated in our vows that it was my job to inspire Doni and that it was Doni's job to provide for and protect me. Twenty years and eight months later I realize that our roles were going to be reversed. It didn't matter though because I would love Doni through anything. "Better or worse" the judge said and I wonder what this situation would be called.

"The end" is what enters my mind and I completely lose it, the tears are uncontrollable again. Doni will be here shortly I remind myself and I have to get it back together. I think of all the impossibilities we had defeated over the years and know that this will be the hardest one yet. I will hold hope until I get told differently but I know that I'm lying to myself. Doni is wheeled back into the room, he is awake but groggy. He sees me, smiles and says "See, I told you it would be okay" and I bow my head and thank God once again.

Doni has another story to tell. My hubby, the continuous storyteller, Stories 101, welcome! He's telling me that one of the members of the surgery staff had been really short tempered and testy with him when she entered the surgery room. Doni, the optimist, tells her he's sorry for having to take her from her bed to come cut his throat and that if he'd been thinking he probably could have saved her a trip if he's just thought to say the right thing to his wife. Surprise, the ultimate betrayer, makes her laugh at the remark and they bond immediately. Even more surprising is that she enters the room while he's telling me the story. He stops to point to her and whispers "She's the one" loud enough for her to hear and the two of them explode in laughter. The woman helps finish the story, and then tells me that she loves my husband's wit, making my heart swell with immense pride.

The woman leaves and Doni and I are holding hands and laughing. I don't know what I'm saying but the words must be right because he's happy and right now that's enough for me. Our happiness is interrupted when a nurse enters the room and tells me I have to leave. The nurse explains that this is ICU and there are rules and tells me that Doni needs time to rest. I want to scream at her that my heart is ripped apart, that she's obviously not human but Doni takes my hand and reassures me he'll be fine. He kisses me, brushes his hand against my cheek and tells me he'll see me in a few hours. Doni doesn't lie I remind myself so I kiss him and leave the room telling him I love him.

My sister is in the waiting room and since we had come so late we hadn't gotten a motel room. It's after 4 am so we decide we will attempt to sleep in my car. I really didn't want to be further away than necessary and figured the hospital parking lot would be close enough. As exhausted as I am, sleep won't come. My mind and heart are still trying to take in all that has happened. This has got to be the worst nightmare I'd ever had, even worse than my snake dream.

I was raised to be terrified of snakes; my grand-mother had been bitten on both legs by copper-heads and the fear trickled down the blood line. Doni and I had watched a show on television about a man that had been wrapped by an anacon-da and he had escaped by scratching the snake's eyes out. Of course I'm trying to escape the snake in my dream and I'm screaming and trying to beat the snake with my fists. Doni, being the protector makes the worst decision of his life; he tries to hold my arms down to keep himself from being hurt. My eyes open just enough to see his bald head and have my fear confirmed that the snake was real. I get my arms away from his grip and try to scratch his eyes out, isn't that what the guy on the show had done? Poor Doni, it wasn't enough I had hurt him but the next day at work he was made fun of by his crew about the "kinky sex" going too far.

The look he returned them stopped them cold but they were more shocked when he said that I had intentionally tried to kill him. Of course he recanted the statement to tell the true story about the dream but I had a "reputation" and

complete fear from everyone for quite some time.
As our married life went on, any sign of a snake
story on television, even an advertisement would
prompt Doni to look at me and say "You're sleeping alone tonight" and we'd both laugh.

Chapter 7

The terror in my heart keep the words repeating over and over; cancer, metastasized, terminal. Haven't we always told each other we could handle the truth better than the unknown? Right now I'm not so sure and I don't want to think where all this leads. My sister is snoring horribly so I get out of the car and go sit in the emergency waiting room trying to make a plan. Me, the constant planner but how do you plan something like this? I start crying and people in the room begin staring at me. Seeing that I'm going nowhere I go back to the car and God in His mercy allows me to sleep, for ninety whole minutes.

I wake up numb and cold not knowing if it's from the November weather or if it's the fear from my heart. Finally I wake my sister up and we go seek out bathrooms so we can wash up and "put our faces on". I realize that I may have to do a lot of that in the future but Doni reads me so well and I don't put on faces; what you see is what you get! How will I ever hide my pain from him so we can attempt happiness through our time left?

Saying a quick prayer I ask God to help me get through all this, even if He has to take me "kicking and screaming" and promise myself that I will not cry in front of Doni because he doesn't need it. Somehow, someway, I am going to find strength so our remaining days will be treasurable and positive. I know where Doni is going when he leaves and I will use that knowledge to help put my needs and feelings to the side, to do what is needed for Doni to live his last days with happiness and never ending love.

Doni and I have not questioned God "Why us?" but have decided we would use our story as an example of the ultimate love people hold in their hearts. There are millions of people that have gone through this story and many millions more that will in the future. "Bring peace to our hearts" I pray, "Even if only temporarily!"

It's still too early to go to the ICU so my sister and I find the cafeteria and try to eat something. We try to talk but what do you say? There will be lots of empty conversations in the future, this is just the first. My cell phone hasn't rung through the night so I know things are okay for now. "Keep those miracles coming" I tell God.

The clock finally says I can see Doni. He looks good and is complaining that they won't let him eat anything because they're going to run tests. Okay, he's grumpy, I can start believing that things are normal and life is good once again.

I ask Doni how his night went and he tells me the nurse had lied to him. Not knowing what he was referring to he finally solved the riddle when he said "I didn't get any sleep, they kept me awake checking me every thirty minutes". Realizing now he's grumpy not from just wanting to eat but lacking in sleep I think to myself that he should be happy he's still alive; I mentally slap myself for the thought. We have little time before the tests start so I begin to work on improving his mood and my thoughts.

When Doni returns from the tests he is in horrible pain, not from the tests but from having to lie down and get back up through each of them. The pain is familiar, he's been hurting for many months and Doni had told me on many occasions that the pain was "killing him". Now I have to add the word "literally" to the phrase.

Doni had been to his personal physician too many times to count, complaining about pain in different areas of his body. The physician had attributed everything to old age and arthritis although Doni was only sixty-seven and had been active all his life. Doni would come home upset and depressed because he knew something was making him hurt and the physician would do no further testing. After one particularly bad visit I finally asked Doni why he didn't change doctors. Doni had replied that he didn't because the only good doctor around our area would be a veterinarian and they wouldn't accept him because he wasn't a horse, cat or dog. We had had a really good laugh over his statement. Doni and his sense of humor!

Chapter 8

Doni and I start preparing ourselves for his family to show up. "Okay God, tall order here, make everyone behave and get along" I silently pray. Doni is just as nervous about the arrivals as I am and he begins telling me the subjects we could talk about and those that are off limits. His list of subjects to remain silent on far outweighs the other list and I wonder if any conversations will happen. Doni tells me we can discuss the weather and maybe follow up with opinions about Santa Claus, but cautiously.

This man lying in the bed here is a really funny guy! I tell Doni that I am really apprehensive and am asking God to keep His hand over my mouth. Doni looks at me then to the ceiling and says "Good luck God, I've been trying for years" and then breaks out laughing. I know how special Doni is and I truly love his humor but I really don't want to share this time with his family and he reads that thought on my face. After all the heartaches these people have caused I don't feel obligated to share any of our time left with them. Doni's wife had died in June of 1987 and we were married in March of 1988 and hell is what we ended up paying for loving each other.

When I heard at work that Doni's wife had died I went to him and asked him how he was holding up and he stated that " Linda had died but I have to go on". I was so impressed with the statement and his determination that my opinion of Doni changed. A few weeks later Doni had come to me and said he needed someone to talk to and asked if I would come to his house. Never thinking twice about telling him yes I agreed to talk to him. We weren't close friends but he knew that I was honest in my beliefs and that I was a good listener. Listening to him that first night blew me away and I found so much that I liked about him.

God took that spark and ran with it. In just a short time we had our first date.

I had never, ever, seen Doni without a hardhat or a welder's cap so I had no clue that he was bald on top of his head. I couldn't contain my reaction in seeing it and said " Oh dear God, you're bald". He looked at me with that special sparkle in his eyes and said " Well yeah, do you still want to go out?" to which I had replied " Well, you are here!" This was one of our favorite stories to tell about our life together. Obviously it worked out in spite of his lack of hair (but we both knew I had enough for both of us and a few more people to spare).

Chapter 9

Doni's family begins to arrive and the tension is thick but I am determined to protect Doni at any cost. As everyone gathers we wait patiently for the test results. Doni's sister-in-law from his first marriage is a nurse and I pull her to the side and ask her to pay special attention to the doctor so she can help us decipher all the information we were going to get.

Finally the group of doctor's comes in the room and I go numb, I'm afraid my legs will give out or worse, that I'd pass out. Here we go I tell my heart, get ready! I am by the bed and I take Doni's hand and he squeezes it. The assigned cancer doctor takes the lead and tells us that the cancer is indeed terminal and that it originated in his kidney. The cancer has spread to his lungs and bones and they've found numerous tumors throughout his body. The cancer has eaten one of his ribs completely gone and is attacking the upper and lower portion of his spine and could collapse which would paralyze him.

"Dear God, how bad does this get?" I ask and the answer is forthcoming…pictures! Oh yes, let's get the visual reality of what's shattering our lives. The pictures show what the doctor has already confirmed starting with his kidney. The picture shows an object that is shaped like a crescent moon and is huge. This isn't the perfect potato shaped kidney most people have.

The pictures keep coming confirming the missing rib, a hip bone that is gone exposing the nerve and the various tumors. I wish that Doni's personal physician was here to explain how arthritis did all this damage. How would the physician react to these pictures being displayed in front of us? Doni had tried so hard to hide all his pain and I wonder now just how much pain he is really in. I check back into the current conversation to hear the doctor explain they don't know what will kill him first; the blood clots are the biggest concern at this time.

Although they've placed a filter in Doni there is still the massive clot between his heart and lungs to be concerned about. I think back to the initial visit Doni had made to complain about his breathing in which he was told it was caused by his being overweight, and then I think about the visit he made concerning his leg. Doni had told his physician that something weird was happening in his leg, a strange feeling, but when he stomped his foot the feeling would quit. Of course the physician had decided Doni was crazy and sent him home. I hadn't known what to make of the situation and remained silent.

The cancer doctor continues to tell us that Doni's cancer is spreading rapidly and could eventually spread to his brain. There is absolute silence in the room and Doni squeezes my hand again signaling me to ask "THE QUESTION", how much longer do we have? Doni's cancer doctor won't give us an answer; he prefers to give his patients hope so they continue fighting. Didn't the doctor use the word terminal? What are we fighting for?

"Time" my heart answers.

The doctors are finished and the family breaks into groups to talk to the various doctors in the room. I feel a hand on my arm and it is one of the doctors. He pulls me aside to a private part of the room and answers "THE QUESTION", six months to two years. I know that my heart stopped at that moment but I keep silent.

I still want to find I'm in a horrible nightmare that I can wake up from. "Cancer" I keep repeating, this just can't be real. You read about it all the time but it happens to other people, not yourself. Doni has already gone through this with his wife and now he is going to experience the same end?

The doctors leave and Doni's family decides to go find something to eat. Finally, some time alone so we can discuss our situation and the future we face. "Doni, you have cancer, what do you think about that?" I say to which he replies "I told you I should have gone to the vet!" We both crack up and are laughing so hard people in the hall are stopping to look into the room. I'm sure they think we're completely crazy, after all this is the cancer ward. No place for laughter right? Wrong! We're going to laugh and love each other till the end. Yes, I said it… the end.

Chapter 10

The doctors consider Doni stable enough to move him out of ICU and I am allowed to stay with him at night but it also allows his family more access to him too. Doni was hearing all the personal fusses between each other and it was upsetting him badly. It was beginning to affect him mentally and physically. The life was literally draining from him.

I'd made a promise to protect Doni at any cost and this was going to be my first necessary attempt. Gathering up all of Doni's family members I took them into the waiting room and unleashed years of anger I'd stored up. I'd never stood up for myself with them, afraid of causing more problems for Doni and his relationships with them. I knew all the pain he'd experienced from it and I drew on that hurt now for my bravery in this altercation.

The "waterloo" started when I told them I wasn't going to allow them to hurt Doni in any way. I informed them that these could be my last days with Doni and I wasn't going to let them ruin them with their pettiness. My "stand" ended by telling them to either get along or go home!

I knew that I had the power to keep them from seeing Doni and at this point I was ready to use my authority because all this backstabbing was exhausting Doni. My anger had exploded and I didn't care what they thought of me at this point. Leaving them all sitting in a state of shock I went to tell Doni what I had done.

I was surprised at myself and somewhat numb when I relayed to Doni what had transpired and was just a little apprehensive as to what his reaction would be. His smile answered the question before he said a single word but he replied "You just go girl!" I guess I'd done well because he was obviously relieved and I could see his face relax. And by the way, the family caravan began with excuses for needing to go home. I was afraid Doni might be upset but he was smiling from ear to ear, he was very glad for what I'd done!

After much discussion with all the doctors involved in Doni's case and knowing that his cancer was so far advanced, we are given three options for treatment in prolonging Doni's life. The first option necessary is to take shots to help dissolve the blood clots. The shots will be administered twice daily in the stomach and Doni can give them to himself.

The second course of action is radiation. It has been recommended that Doni have ten days of treatment, not for the cancer but to help eliminate some of his pain. Doni will get to choose which spots they concentrate on to which he immediately replies "Just do all of me!" Doni has never allowed me the true knowledge of his level of pain but his statement now is a true indication that Doni is in horrible pain.

The last option given is for Doni to take an immune therapy drug. The choices are limited to but a handful and their success rates of extending someone's life don't add up to much more than a year, IF IT WORKS!

Okay, time for a new plan. Sign me up, Dani the constant planner. After little discussion we make the decision to try all three options and alter each as we find how Doni does with them. It will be up to Doni to weigh the side effects versus the treatment result and I can only sit on the sideline and make notes to his doctors as to what I see personally.

Okay, decision made, let's get on with it!

Okay, decision stalled already! We've made phone calls to our insurance company who has declined two of our options. The first is the shots for the blood clots. So began every person's nightmare and the fight is on! We finally get agreement for us to get enough injections through the hospital to get Doni through a few weeks. The battle will continue but for now we'll be covered.

The second denial is for the immune therapy drug. Sitting in the doctors insurance liaisons office I learn that this drug is over $13,000 a month and our portion will be just over $2,600 per month. My mouth gaps open from the shock not to mention my heart is now at shoe level. I explain to the insurance liaison that the amount is crazy and we can't afford it (while my mind is clicking through options of selling our house and taking our retirement money out of our 401k).

The liaison explains that there are several agencies that help finance such situations and we could fill out paperwork to apply for them. There is no option here, I lay my head on the woman's desk and bawl loud enough that everyone in the clinic can hear me.

"How will I tell Doni?" my heart cries. I fill out the applications as Doni's sister sits beside me and when done we go back to the hospital. I go into Doni's room alone to tell the man I love that I've failed him.

"Flex those muscles" I tell myself, "Here we go!" I sit next to Doni's bed and explain what I have learned and he takes my hand and gently tells me "It's okay Dani, I don't need the medicine!" "Yes you do!" I scream back and begin to cry. He squeezes my hand, looks me in the eyes and tells me that everything will be okay. The doctor comes in, sees I've fallen apart and after hearing the story tells us that they'd get something worked out. "Too late" I think, "I've already panicked, already questioned God's ability to help us".

Chapter 11

HOME! Just for the weekend but we get to go home to our security, to our comfort zone, to normalcy. "Not anymore" I have to remind myself. The drive home is heavenly. We've run the first stretch and succeeded. Doni is taking notice of the surroundings through new eyes, new outlook? Doesn't this hurt him to know it may be the last time he sees it? I won't ask him, the truth would be too much to bear. He gets really quiet and I'm afraid he's reading my thoughts through my face. He turns to look at me and his face is horribly serious. "Quick" I tell myself, "lighten things back up; I don't want to cry in front of him".

Nothing comes! The old mind has gone completely blank! "Dani", he says, "Don't let my kids screw you". My shock is apparent and he acknowledges it. He wants me to go over our will with him. His questions begin and my heart breaks with every one of them. We have always been honest with each other and I know in his questions that he is trying to tell me he knows he will die but I answer every one of them honestly. Doni knows his predicted lifespan told by the doctor because I had told him and I remind him now that we could still have lots of time. "We'll have time" he agrees "But I need to be sure you'll be okay".

I want to scream! Not at Doni, it wouldn't be fair but we both know our lives will never be okay again. When Doni leaves, my life will be over. "God, please let me go with him when he leaves, I don't want to know life without him" I cry inside my heart. "A miracle is what we need here; could we have a really big one, the ultimate one?" I ask God.

We get home to spend a beautiful weekend together determined to deal the best we can with everything that comes to us. Doni and I have promised to be honest and talk openly about everything, no holds barred. I know it will be difficult for both of us but we will do it! We've never had problems talking in the past but the topics had been easier; a lot easier!

Back to Salt Lake, the weekend flew by so quickly. We've been given hospital housing for the two weeks we'll be here for the radiation treatments at only $25 a night. The only problem is the steps in front of the house; they're hard for someone with a walker. God, what were we thinking? Doni's been using a walker to assist him with walking for months. What's up with this? Can't we add two and two?

Denial has to be the reason. Everything we'd been through with Doni's health we had chalked up to Lyme's disease. He'd been diagnosed with an advanced stage of it several years earlier. We believed this was what had been debilitating him in his walking. Again in this prognosis Doni had been to the local physician saying that he was going to die if they didn't find what was wrong with him.

The physician, exhausted with Doni, had told him there was only Lyme's Disease left to check for and Wyoming didn't have that type of ticks. Doni had forced the physician to test him and when the test came back it was of course positive. The guilt sets in now that all this time Doni had had cancer and I hadn't seen it. I'm not a doctor I remind myself, but it is of little help in relieving what I feel. There's a powerful need inside me to blame Doni's physician for his lack of interest. There had never been any mention to the Lyme's disease in all these latest complaints, instead diagnosing Doni with old age and arthritis. It was a lazy way out I believe but I can still put a certain amount of guilty blame to myself.

The radiation is horrible for Doni and he wants to quit the first day because the pain in lying down and getting up is beyond his capacity to handle. I turn into Doni's personal cheerleader and remind him of the final results, less pain. On the third day of radiation Doni starts peeing blood and passing blood clots through his urine.

Doni is scared and I am worse but I won't let him see it. This is the beginning of many emergency calls and the beginning of a new, stronger edition of me. I have to be strong to keep him calm as well as keeping myself calm. I've never seen weakness in Doni before so I have to excuse myself and take a walk outside to cry. I don't want Doni to hear me. "Still got my back God?" I ask because I really want to pass out from all this hurt.

We get through this current episode and now begin concentrating on Christmas. "Please, please let us be home this Christmas; it may be our last one together" I beg. No tree, no presents will be given but I don't care. Nothing interests me in the season but to spend it with Doni, at home! "To hell with everything else" I tell myself. Did I really say this out loud? Guess I did but surely God understands my frustration right now. "Sorry God" I say; just in case!

This time in my life has got to be the hardest period I've ever encountered, my energy is gone and I can't sleep. Too much to think about, too much getting up to help Doni through the night, too little time to watch his face while he's unaware I'm doing it. It's getting harder for Doni to get up and down out of a chair so I have to step in. "I'm not complaining Lord" I explain, "I'm just broken". "Do you see how much he hurts and how much it destroys him to have to depend on me for things?" I cry out. Faith tells me that God knows my heart and can see how many pieces it is in at this point. Can most people even count this high I wonder? I know I can't! There's no time for this pity party and I tell myself to get on with things.

The radiation is over, we get to go home...BEFORE CHRISTMAS!

Chapter 12

Our drive home is filled with conversation; our time has been shortened so we feel the need to say everything we can now. How many people experience the closeness we have found during this time? Why did it take cancer to throw off the inhibitions of daily life and to see what's truly important? This thought is one of the saddest I have questioned so far.

We get to the house and find that it's been cleaned by some of my friends from work and the Christmas tree has been put up. Doni and I can't contain our feelings so we sit crying, holding hands, looking at our tree. The tree doesn't hold our personal ornaments but ones that have been lovingly handmade and others that were bought by my girlfriends.

"See honey, there is good in the world" I tell him as we take in all the sights to add to our cherished memories. The phone rings and interrupts our thoughts. On the line is one of the girls telling us that the people at work have taken up a collection and have purchased dinner for Doni, me and my entire family. They knew we'd not had time to make any plans and was bringing us our "Christmas Dinner".

Several people from work show up with trays of prime rib, turkey and all the extras. Doni can't control his tears as I help take everything to the kitchen. How good God has been to us with people in our lives, very special people! After all the trays are delivered we sit in the living room to chat for a brief time and are handed an envelope with money. "What have we done to deserve all this?" I question as Doni grabs my hand and begins to sob, tears streaking down his face. Doni is the reason for all these blessings I remind myself, his kindness to everyone throughout his life has come back home. The love we are experiencing is immeasurable, never ending and perfect. "Thank you God!" I say.

After our friends leave I hold Doni's hand and watch tears fall from his face and am reminded of his perfect, tender heart. How can I ever tell him how thankful I am for his love that has no boundaries, for the man in him that loves without question and who sees love for what it truly is? I can't say anything right now but together holding hands we release ourselves of our heartfelt tears.

Doni had always played "Mr. Tough Guy" but I knew all along what a softie he really was. I tried hard to keep his secret but he kept letting it out of the bag. Not my fault right? Doni had always stopped to help people on the highway that was having car problems and was always giving money to people asking for handouts. Doni's heart was beyond generous and we had acquired many friends from his acts of kindness. We took strangers into our home and I never questioned a lack of judgment on his part.

Helping others had become the norm for us and when I stopped to help a family that had wrecked on the ice Doni went with me to the hospital to check on them. As each member of the family was released I would take them home and Doni would care for them while I sat at the hospital. Doni lovingly made breakfast for them the next morning while they awaited the arrival of a family member to get them. I couldn't have loved him more and was thankful for my "Tough Guy"!

Christmas turns out to be very emotional for both of us. Doni is upset that he hadn't got me a gift, putting me first as always. I explain to him that he was wrong; I had received two of the best presents ever this year, having him and being home for Christmas. Trying to lighten our moods he adorns himself with a Christmas bow and models it for me from a sitting position. I couldn't keep it inside and cracked up with laughter at his antics. What a fool he could make of himself! He recounted to me another Christmas story long past where my daughter had decorated him with Christmas bows and I actually found the picture later to prove his story. In the back of my mind I continually ask myself if this would be our last Christmas together, I'm human and can't help myself. I wonder if Doni thinks the same thing but again I won't ask because his answer may rip my heart out.

Chapter 13

We begin preparations for a trip back to Salt Lake for Doni's first doctor's appointment of the year. We've been told that we have been denied assistance for his medicine because we make too much money. My cell phone has become a permanent attachment to my body from trying to deal with our insurance company.

I had tried to "play nice" as Doni would remind me before each phone call but I wasn't always successful. In one conversation I shocked the insurance representative by giving her my address and told her to bring the knife to kill my husband and get it over with. Another representative received a threat that I was going to ask God not to let her have another night's sleep because she was denying me more time with my husband, time we wanted desperately! I felt shame in my words but not for long, the shame was placed back on them, the heartless people that God must cry over!

Our doctor has little new information but asks why we haven't started the drugs. We explain to him as honestly as we can that we were still fighting the insurance company and that we couldn't afford them on our own. He tells us there are agencies to help and we reply by telling him we were denied because we made too much money. The doctor tells us to stay where we are and leaves the room. When he returns he has another insurance liaison with him who asks questions and then the doctor tells her to go figure something out. We are stunned but so willing for any help in the matter.

The doctor continues in explaining what each monthly visit will entail including x-rays, cat scans and possible MRI's. Doni groans at the thought of having to go through them but they are a must in determining the progress of Doni's cancer. We get interrupted when the insurance liaison comes in to tell us that our insurance will pay AND that both medications will only cost us $40.00 each per month! Doni grabs my hand and without thought we both burst into tears. Another miracle! Isn't God awesome?

I had gone as a teenager to the North American Christian Convention in St. Louis, Missouri. One of the sessions I attended was about prayer. I can't remember the presenters name but he told us that our prayers were answered more often than we realize. The man had said that we ask for too many things and are too busy to pay attention for God's answer. He'd challenged us to write down our prayer requests for each month and review them. No surprise, he was right! How humanly selfish we have become I had thought then and still do.

God's blessings to us through all this are so powerful they are recognized immediately and there is no need to make a list. No questions about them, no hesitation. Even with our doubts God overlooks our weaknesses to show His greatness! Thank God!

Chapter 14

Our next visit to the doctor finds Doni in really bad shape. He has been having trouble talking, can't concentrate or think straight, is combative and even worse is being verbally abusive to me. In fear of retribution I still tell Doni's doctor the changes in his symptoms and as predicted Doni unleashes on me. The doctor tries to intervene, only to find himself in the hot seat along with me. I can see the look in his eyes when he excuses himself from the room. I feel abandoned and wonder what the doctor was doing to have left me alone with this madman.

In little time my answer comes when the door flies open and two hospital attendants enter with a wheelchair, Doni is being readmitted to the hospital. Doni becomes scared and I am confused but try to comfort Doni during the walk across to the hospital from the cancer clinic.

After running many tests we are told that Doni's cancer has begun to take the calcium out of his bones and depositing it in his bloodstream which is life threatening. Doni is given a blood transfusion, three pints of blood. "Am I leaking" he asks? I have to shake my head in disbelief to his question. The nurse laughs and looks around his bed and tells him she doesn't see anything. Doni relaxes and I have to laugh at their escapades. Doni will now have to take monthly IV treatments to deal with this latest find but relief comes when they tell us the insurance company will pay for it. For once, no fighting!

Doni improves quickly and begins bugging the hospital staff with stories of his hunting and fishing trips. I sit listening to them, trying to commit them to my memory somewhere. I silently watch him, listening to his words and his voice. I watch the light flickering in his eyes as he anticipates the reaction of each person listening to the story. I know that I will never tell Doni goodbye, I swear this as I think of how much I love his eyes, the mirror to his soul.

What a beautiful place is reflected in them. I feel so much love and admiration for this man, my lover and my best friend. Although our intimacy disappeared sexually before we learned of the Lyme's disease, I didn't care. Love has other venues of intimacy. Doni is still the love of my life and I feel his love through holding his hand, can see it through his eyes and hear it in his voice. It's like someone who loses one of their senses and they compensate that loss with the other senses that are left. I'm thankful for Doni just sharing his life with me!

Knowing that Doni won't be selfish through this journey I realize that all cancer patients must be this way. If you want to see the face of hope, visit a cancer clinic. There are no strangers admitted, everyone is family and encouragement is truly endless. I have never once seen tears in the clinic, only strength and determination. People diagnosed with cancer find normal lives taken away and replaced with a new world of "unlimited unknowns" yet they are driven. Fear is a horrible evil but in a cancer clinic fear is put aside while everyone present is relearning life and living hope.

Doni sees me watching him and he smiles. I smile back because I know that Doni is content at the moment and that alone makes me happy. A new shift of the nursing staff has started and story time begins again!

Chapter 15

Homebound again! We have succeeded in facing another hurdle and overcoming it. The worst part of our lives now has to be leaving Doni when I go to work. Most times he is by himself and my heart rips at the thought of his loneliness or that he may be gone before I get home. How would I ever live with myself if it really happened? I continually beg God to let Doni die at home, in my arms, with just the two of us here. Not only do I feel guilty for leaving Doni alone, I feel guilty for needing a rest from him too. I hate watching his body wither away but am so grateful that his spirit is still strong. I'm human; doing what I can to survive I keep telling myself but the thought doesn't help much!

My co-workers have been donating personal time so I am never lacking a paycheck. How much more wonderful can a group of people be? This question is easily answered; they hold me when my tears flow at work. Going to work offers me a chance to breath, time to plan the next step and the ability to cry freely. I won't cry in front of Doni because it hurts him and he doesn't need it.

One of my co-workers told me he hated to hear me cry because I didn't cry from my heart, I cried from my soul. I take it as a compliment because when I offer my heart I give it freely, wholly and forever. Doni is the love of my life and we've had a pretty good marriage despite the rocky start with our families. I had been put on a pedestal which scared me; I'm afraid of heights you know!

My life had never encountered this type of love but God knew what He was doing when he brought us together. I had written Doni a poem after our first year together and told him we complimented and completed each other. Doni knew that he was the first and only person in my life that I trusted completely and this truly meant something to him! Doni is my comfort zone, my security, and my "hope". Now this will all be gone and I feel another rip of the heart.

How many roads can a mind wonder down? I'm exhausting myself mentally, physically and spiritually. Cancer isn't just attacking my husband, it's attacking me too! I get so tired from the sleepless nights, taking care of Doni's needs, getting him up and down from his chair, the late night talks when Doni needs to be assured of things bothering him. I have to remain strong, anything less would be unfair to him. Doni needs his strength to have more time for us. I told Doni that I would help him fight until he told me he couldn't fight anymore. Is this love or craziness? Sometimes there are such thin lines between them.

Another visit to the doctor and we are told the immune therapy drug is working. "Did you hear that honey?" I ask. "Time, we've bought more time". I don't care how much, I'll take every day, hour and minute. "Please don't let him leave too soon" I beg God, "I'm not ready yet". I'll never be ready and that smile on his face means everything to me. He takes my hand and the world is right again!

Chapter 16

Happiness, we're together...still! People are starting to visit and Doni loves the company, they fill his mind with something other than pain, medicine and me. People can be so kind and uplifting and others can be so cruel. One of Doni's friends comes to the house so drunk he can't stand up. It's embarrassing to Doni and he's heart-broken. I am mad and want to beat the man sober. The friend keeps hitting Doni on his arm causing horrible pain and is swearing at Doni because he won't go drive his car. I try to explain that Doni can hardly walk but the man won't listen. I want to call the sheriff and have him arrested, Doni shows compassion as usual. Doni makes him stay while he sobers up enough to leave. I stay mad because I'll cry if I don't. Doni whispers to me "Play nice Dani" and this one time I want to choke him for saying it. Instead I reply "Sometimes I hate it when you're right!" and he laughs at me.

Things are getting hard as Doni realizes how little he can do and begins to call himself "worthless". I spend lots of hours telling him that his physical contributions may be limited but his other contributions are not. I begin to see the light drain from his eyes and I am desperate to do whatever it takes to fight it back. I encourage Doni to tell me stories, to explain something to me we're watching on television and finally I decide I have to get his friends involved.

There are little things around the house that need done so his friends and I make a pact to be schemers to help improve Doni's opinion of himself. I hate scheming, going behind his back, but I will do everything necessary to encourage Doni to keep going. Over a period of time each friend involved shows up to "visit" and in the course of the conversation ask Doni if there's anything they can help him do.

At this point I would mention one of the little jobs needing done and they would tell Doni "Let's go look at it". Doni would get packed to the job to help look over the situation. Heavy discussion would take place in making a plan and the job would get done with Doni as the boss and the friend being the laborer. Doni had been a boss at his job in Oregon and his reputation was of being fair and honest with everyone. I see the light coming back on and the "worthlessness" talk gets dropped. Life is good, Doni felt useful again!

Each new visit to the doctor shows that Doni's immune therapy drug is working and the cancer has slowed its progression. We have more time I keep thinking; let's make the most of it. Doni is feeling good enough to go for drives. I know his pain is limitless but we drug him up before we take off so he can get out of the house. Doni wants fresh air, a renewal of life however temporary it may be. One trip is a few hours long and he wants to get out and look around. I talk him out of it because I just didn't want to watch him hurt. I will always feel guilty for that decision but I'll have to live with it.

Doni's pain is getting worse so we make a trip to the radiation doctor in Salt Lake to discuss if Doni can have more treatments. We are sitting in the room and when he enters both Doni and I see "That look!" The doctor immediately looks down at the papers and Doni tells him "Go ahead and say it!" The doctor explains he never expected Doni to live more than a few weeks after his first radiation session and is totally surprised to see him. Doni laughs, I smile and the doctor relaxes but is still a little embarrassed. Honesty is required here and laughter too. We are told Doni can have no more radiation; his pain medication will have to be increased. Doni expresses his fear of becoming a drug addict and now it's the doctor's turn to laugh. It is explained once again that cancer patients CANNOT become drug addicts as their systems are different from normal systems.

So much information to be learned through this ordeal, what is it they say about knowledge? It's the key to something...in our case it's called survival! Doni and I have been on the computer constantly looking at information about his cancer, the symptoms and possible treatments. Each new medicine, each new treatment available gets researched endlessly so we aren't unarmed when we see the doctors.

Unknown to Doni is that I continue my research at work on websites for caregivers and what will happen in his last days. Hospice is mentioned continually but Doni has refused their services so far, his memory is still fresh from when his wife Linda had died from cancer. He wasn't ready to concede yet that his lifetime was short and I wasn't going to force it. "Hope" they say… number one strategy in cancer patients.

Chapter 17

Doni is starting to get more tired and his appetite is changing. I can't convince myself that the cancer isn't spreading but how can I know without "really knowing"? I don't want any bad news; we've been doing so well. "Please God let it continue" I pray. We sit down for dinner, Doni's daughter and son-in-law are present when Doni looks at me and announces "I don't like chicken!" He says this so childlike but so seriously and we are all lost for words.

"Okay" I tell him, "I'll fix you something else". He's starting to become a lot to handle but I will never put him in a home. It's like dealing with a 2-year old at times and it breaks my heart. I'm still resolved to not let Doni see me cry. "Later" I keep telling myself, when I'm alone. I compare myself to Scarlet in Gone with the Wind; "I'll think about it tomorrow" she had said but in my case tomorrow is never going to come. I'm realizing that both Doni and I are in pain, his is physical and mine is mental.

Six months! We've made it to the first marker. Things seem to be somewhat good but the new tests will tell us more. The doctor tells us that things are basically the same, a couple of new spots in the lungs and a couple of initial spots have grown but not much. This tells us that Doni's immune therapy drug is still working. "Yes" he whispers to me. Doni takes my hand and it is shaking, I hope that he doesn't feel mine doing the same.

Our conversation on the drive home reflects our good news and Doni is giving me his list of things he's thankful for. He's put me at the top and it humbles me. I never dreamed that we'd be experiencing all this nor would I have imagined that Doni was transferring his strength over to me. I would never have made it this far without that strength and it is one of the strangest thoughts I'd had so far.

We sit down to dinner, again his daughter and son-in-law are here when Doni announces this time "I hate beef!" "What's up with this?" I wonder but I get up and fix him something else to eat. Doni's appetite is continuously changing and I appease his cravings without question. I feel lucky that he's still eating. Payday candy bars, ice cream, oatmeal, cereal, Gatorade. Whatever he wants he will have!

My exhaustion is becoming really apparent. My co-workers keep telling me to take time off but Doni won't let me. Every day I take off is being supplemented with someone else's personal time. I know how tired I am, as does Doni but I tell everyone that I am fine and keep going. I've never been a quitter and I'm not going to start now.

Doni won't answer the phone and it puts me in a panic. "God, please let him be okay!" I ask. "Don't let him die alone!" I add.

I find a friend of ours in the vicinity and tell him to go in the house and call me. He finds Doni coma-like but he's beginning to come out of it. Of course Doni won't let him take him to the hospital and he won't let me come home. So typical of Doni!

Before Doni was diagnosed with the Lyme's disease he had had two incidents that sent me in a tizzy. The first was when he was traveling to Oregon and he'd taken the camp trailer so he could stay for a while. Not hearing from him one night sent me in a rage until I heard from him the next day, he'd been overtaken by the heat and had spent the night face first on the ground where he'd passed out.

The second incident he had called me at work and his first words were "Don't panic" which of course made me panic." I fell down" he tells me. "Are you hurt?" I respond. "Not bad, I'll quit bleeding eventually" he says. I tell him I'm coming home and he gets mad so I question him further as to his condition. He's bleeding from his head and fingers and tells me he's using a paper towel to rub the bone in his finger back into place." It looks kind of weird" he'd told me. When I arrived home I'd found blood everywhere in the garage from the split in his head and his broken finger. He had no idea why he fell, didn't remember the actual fall and refused to go to the hospital, as usual!

I've called and set up an emergency visit to Doni's doctor in Salt Lake and it's discovered that his blood sugar is out of sorts. Just one more worry to add to the already long list. We spend several nights up while we get his sugar counts adjusted and steady. I'm totally exhausted now, empty is in the rearview mirror.

Doni's humor comes shining through and he has me laughing in spite of my exhaustion. Doni is adamant that all our talks take place at the dining room table. It's so hard to get him there but I'll do it to make him happy. Waiting to see what the topic will be, or how many will be discussed, is like gambling without money. The most rewarding payouts seem to be during the night and in the first hours of the morning. I don't know if Doni's clock is off but I treasure any time he is awake and we can talk.

Doni has also started having fevers every afternoon about the same time. You can watch his cheeks develop the dark red which quickly spreads up his head and down his neck. The doctor explains that these are what are known as "tumor fevers". What will they think of next we wonder?

Doni and I both know our time is getting shorter but we don't waste time letting it destroy us. We spend every moment possible sharing our memories of the life we put together. Our jigsaw puzzle is coming together and will soon be finished. I have always loved working jigsaw puzzles and Doni, my constant joker, would steal a piece and hide it so he'd always be the one to finish it. I know that when he dies he will again play the last piece and finish the challenge but this time he will actually be that piece. "Just let this puzzle be the most beautiful we've ever put together" I ask God.

Doni and I had been working an especially difficult puzzle which was stumping both of us. Doni was ready to quit but of course I always have to finish what I've started no matter what. One night after a few hours of challenge Doni had said out loud "And I thought you drove me crazy!" I was ready to give him a real tongue lashing when he quickly intercepted and said " I said thought remember, not that you really do!" I'd lost the battle without one single word!" So Doni: I thought!

Chapter 18

D oni is sleeping more and his pain is increasing quickly. At this time Doni is taking 180 mg of oxycontin. The doctor has told us that 60 mg would kill a normal person. Doni explains to him that he's been anything but normal since marrying me. "Very funny" I tell him but it's made the doctor laugh. Doni worries that someone will break into our house to get his medicine so I only put out enough for a few days and lock the rest up in our safe.

Doni's family is coming at times to help out and I'm so thankful because it allows me to go to work and not worry so much. Doni is experiencing more problems with his thinking and it makes him mad if things are too complicated for him to comprehend. He's showing impatience towards our grandson Bailey, the "love of our lives".

I see the pain in Doni's face when Bailey hugs him but they're "best buds". Doni sits Bailey down and explains that he is really hurting so their hugs will have to be gentle now. Doni and I won't tell Bailey that Doni is going to die from his illness. I go outside so they can have some special time and I have to cry. I don't want to think about how Bailey will handle life without his Papa.

Bailey lives with his paternal grandparents who have custody of him. They'd taken him from my daughter and their son when he was only five months old. He's now eight years old. We also have a granddaughter Morgan who was adopted by her paternal grandparents (different from Baileys) and before the signature was dry they'd taken away all our rights to see her after they'd promised they wouldn't. Doni and I hired a lawyer to fight but we lost because of the laws of Wyoming. It had devastated both of us and I'd had a nervous breakdown and wanted to die.

Doni is talking more and more about Morgan now and keeps telling me how sorry he is about the whole mess. Doni hates when I'm unhappy but he seems to be cleansing his soul of guilt he feels. He talks more about his funeral and things that need to be done before he dies. I hate all these discussions but I've promised to love Doni through this and to help any way I can to make things easier for him. My dad had passed away just a couple of months before we discovered Doni had cancer. My family had spent a night sorting through pictures to use for a DVD of my dad's life to play at the viewing. Doni hadn't been feeling good (even way back then I remember now) but when I got home he'd watched the DVD and had told me he wanted one made for his funeral.

How little we knew how soon I'd be making one! I can't work on the DVD in front of Doni so I work on it while he sleeps. Doni knows what I'm doing and tells me he trusts my judgment. It's hard work for my heart but I'll do it for Doni.

It's time for the next doctors visit and Doni informs me he can't do it, the pain is too great to travel. "Oh God no, not now" I pray but I bite my tongue and keep my composure. I have to make phone calls to see what options we have. I call Salt Lake first and tell the cancer clinic the situation with Doni. We are told that we'll have to find a local doctor that will work with their office.

I'd rather get bit by a snake then do this but okay, here we go again! I make more calls than I can count, researching doctors, asking questions, finding our next miracle. Of course God supplies one and we find a physician's assistant that will take on our situation. A woman who is studying internal medicine, just what we'd asked for.

Doni asks me at dinner that night what time we have to leave for Salt Lake and I'm stunned. I remind him that he'd told me he couldn't travel and he doesn't remember it and gets upset. How fast a floor can fall from underneath you and when you land you realize the truth, the end is coming sooner than you're ready for. I don't have time for pity so I give the situation over to God and ask him to handle it for me.

Thankfully Doni decides he needs to rest and I get him back to his chair and he's quickly asleep. I look at the chair, a cherished memory from our co-workers. I'd taken some of the money they'd collected to buy a chair that electronically lifts a person to help them get up and down. "My chair of love" Doni had named it. I excuse myself to the computer room to work on Doni's DVD for his funeral and the tears come. My heart is ripping apart and I can actually hear it in my sobbing. "Hope, where are you?" I ask, "This is not the time to play hide and seek." "God please don't let me see the truth, it's too much to bear" I cry.

I can't sleep as there is too much pain from my heart breaking but this time the pain is real, I question if I'm having a heart attack. I beg God to let me live long enough to get Doni through this journey and then He can have me. I also beg God again to let Doni leave while in my arms with just the two of us there and I finally cry myself to sleep.

Chapter 19

We have our first visit with the new doctor who Doni lovingly calls Dr. Amy. She's been given copies of all Doni's reports which fill a folder big enough to use as a door-stop. Doni is mesmerized with the new doctor and can't talk from staring. Not only is she beautiful but she has a ring in her tongue he can't quit watching. She finds it funny as do I and we all have a laugh. Dr. Amy is great with Doni and when he asks the same question over and over (not remembering he's already asked it) she answers him like it's the first time he's asked. She's hired! She's perfect!

Discussion is made about other forms of pain medication and she emphasizes that Doni doesn't have to suffer. Doni hates drugs, still afraid he'll become an addict. I can see his pain is horrible and getting worse but Doni doesn't give in easily. His oxycontin is increased again and I wonder how much more he can take without it killing him. Doni's list of medicines is so long now that I have to make a schedule on a chalkboard and I carry a copy in my purse that I made on the computer, along with a living will.

After Doni's surgery for the blood clot filter we were instructed to see a lawyer and get a living will and a power of attorney to carry with us at all times. Not something most people would think about but then cancer patients are different. This is one of the items considered "necessary" through the journey. I thought it would be hard at the lawyer's office but Doni was determined to make it as painless as possible for me and we walked out of the office with not only what we needed but with a sense of security and peace of mind. No problems, piece of cake!

We find ourselves with another visit to the local emergency room. Doni had given himself an injection and it had been bleeding for three days. "I'm leaking again" he'd said but it wasn't leaking, it was pumping out blood. No panic, just another episode of disbelief in what we could experience in all this. There have been so many physical issues, mental issues and changes to our lives but the greatest experience in all this was the closeness we'd found. I asked Doni if he thought all cancer patients experienced the same bond and he replied that to get through the struggle of cancer it had to be there.

We're sitting in the room at the hospital waiting for the emergency room doctor to come in and the bleeding stops, after three days. Doni looks at me and says "Just our luck huh". The doctor on call walks in and Doni states "Boy are you good, the bleeding stopped already!" Doni's body is changing rapidly and he'd hit an artery with the needle. Before this incident

Doni had injected himself a few times to find the needle had popped right back out. Doni had said "Did you see that?" and while laughing explained to me that his fat was turning into rubber. As I said before, my two year old at play!

There is something growing on Doni's neck now, growing rapidly and is black. Is it cancer? Back to see Dr. Amy. She explains that they could do a biopsy but if Doni wasn't having any pain with it she would recommend leaving it alone. She talks to us for a long time. Doni wants her attention and she gives it to him, gladly. Doni always hugs her neck as we leave but I do too. When we're hugging though she is whispering that she will call me later which means there is information she doesn't want to share with Doni.

Dr. Amy and I have formed a secret pact, one to protect Doni and keep him hopeful so he'll fight harder. Both of us have seen Doni's frustration in trying to interpret his issues and she understands that I want to protect him from as much as I can. Doni's time on earth may be limited but it will be filled with only good things and I'll keep the bad to myself.

Chapter 20

Doni isn't feeling well and spends more time sleeping. I keep wondering what comes next and panic I won't recognize the end but am guaranteed by all the medical staff that I will know. I make private calls from work to Salt Lake and Dr. Amy to keep informed as to what is going on and how best to help Doni. I may think I'm keeping things from him but he'd experienced this journey with his first wife and he knows, he's just not saying anything to protect me. My plan for now is denial, I'll take it all in, store it in memory for later and then Scarlet and I can think about it tomorrow.

Doni's pain is so bad today that he's crying. I didn't think I had any heart left to get ripped out but I was so wrong! I call Dr. Amy and she works us in. This time she easily convinces Doni that he should start on the pain patch. She also believes that new tests are required to find out what is going on. Doni dreads them so much but he knows they're necessary to tell us what we need to do.

Still a fighter, I can only thank God for Doni's will. A scan for Doni gets scheduled for the next morning. I spend the day with a bad case of premonition. "Please God, let me be wrong!"

I beg. We show up for the appointment and I kiss Doni before they take him back. I want to find a place to hide so I can cry out my fear but can find no such place!

After only fifteen minutes the technician comes out to tell me Doni is too large for the machine and they had got him stuck and he'd panicked. They bring him out in a wheelchair; he's white as a ghost and shaking uncontrollably. I run to him and grab his hand.

"I couldn't breathe" he tells me in a 2-year olds voice. He's shaken up and I try to calm him. "I almost died" he cries with actual tears coming from his eyes. I am furious with the technician at the moment and I'm hurt and scared for Doni. He's always been so strong in handling situations and I realize that those times are gone. I know this is a very bad sign but my need to comfort him overpowers the thought. Okay master planner, what now?

The only place available for the scan is in Salt Lake for the next day. Doni can't travel, isn't that why we're seeing Dr. Amy? I discuss the situation with Doni and he tells me he can make it. Unbelievable this roller coaster ride we're on. Doni and I sit at the dining room table discussing everything when he gets deathly quiet.

With fear taking over I ask him, "What is it honey?" With innocence and urgency he responds "You need to write a book, please promise me all this won't be for nothing!"

He wants me to write a book? I've never written anything more than a poem. "That's a tall order honey but if it's what you want I'll try…for you". He's compiling a list for me to write down and tells me to keep track of things so I don't forget. "We can worry about that later" I tell him but he's adamant that I could forget. How could you possibly forget any of this I think? It's been the journey of a lifetime and I'm not much of a traveler. I'm happiest at home, in my comfort zone. Yes, I still remember it. I want to have it back.

I can't sleep again. My heart and mind are having a huge battle. I'm so scared right now. "Lean on me" God keeps telling me but I can't, not right now. I want to, really I do but…

We drug Doni up and hopefully he'll be okay on our trip. He tries to sleep but the pain is too bad. "We were surviving, what happened?" I ask myself. My heart and mind are too tired to invite faith and trust. The battle last night was more than I can bear and I need a second wind. I need good news; I need Doni back the way he was before!

The technician in Salt Lake is filling us in on the procedure, like we've never done this before. Okay, let him tell us, we're listening. Doni gets wheeled away and the emptiness I experience feels like betrayal. I know the end is coming but I don't want to accept it. Yes they told us he's terminal, I've seen first-hand how his body has changed. I've seen him cry from his pain, I've heard confusion in his words. I've changed my mind God, I'm begging for help in accepting what's to come". I see the technician coming with "that look" on his face.

Oh God, not another one I think. "We've had a little accident" he tells me. "Your husband misjudged the height of the bed to the floor and fell but he's okay, just a little shaken up" he says as he turns to leave. He's gone back to get Doni and I sit stunned, Doni gets stuck in the first machine, falls off the second machine, just what is the plan for the final encore? Doni arrives in a wheelchair and he's laughing like there's no tomorrow. I can't help myself and tell him "What some people won't do for attention!" Doni and the technician begin laughing harder and I join in. Laughter feels so good in these moments, so much better than the alternative.

We have time to kill before our visit with the cancer doctor so we sit in the waiting room and the storyteller begins. GOOD FOR HIM! We couldn't waste a trip to Salt Lake so we'd asked to see the doctor while we're here for Doni's scan. Without the test results there's not much the doctor can do except listen to our concerns about Doni's new symptoms.

We ask if Doni can change his immune therapy drug and I ask about the new one that had just been approved. The doctor is stunned but I'd done my homework. "I may be computer challenged but I'm not computer illiterate" I explain. I can stumble through just about anything especially when it's as important as Doni's life.

The doctor suggests a different drug and I refuse his suggestion telling him that reports show it's the least productive drug. Doni's chest swells with pride as I argue with the doctor, it's written all over his face. Doni hates computers, had originally refused to turn one on but I believe he's changed his mind now, maybe a little! Our computer is a link to our decisions we make throughout this whole ordeal and has helped us make them intelligently. The decision is made to wait until all the test results come back from today. No sense in changing things if we don't have to.

Chapter 21

With nothing learned we head for home. Doni talks the whole way home, he has much to get out. He looks at the scenery and points things out to me. He's seeing the surroundings as though it's his last look. I almost wreck the car with this thought but Doni doesn't say anything. We have learned to talk openly, without hesitation; no time for leaving things out now. I am going to help Doni in his transfer from earth to heaven, there's time for pity later Scarlet. I wish that I could see the beauty Doni is explaining. Is he getting glimpses of heaven I wonder?

I wish I could feel in my heart what he's experiencing. I'd trade places with him in less than a heartbeat. I look at this man and see the love he's brought me over the years. I recognize the knowledge he's taught me and remember the library of stories he's told over the years.

Doni has asked me several times if I'll be okay after he's gone. I'm clueless to what I'll be when he leaves me. Just for a few moments at times have I allowed myself to think outside my comfort zone but I can't imagine a life without Doni. Where's that master planner when you need them? I can't think about his actual death, I can only come up with projects around the house to fill my empty days after Doni's gone.

I spend another sleepless night feeling impending doom with the test results. I thank God again that my co-workers have donated time so I can be with Doni. I would gladly do without a check but Doni's argument is that I need my job after he's gone. I hate thinking of Doni in the past tense and I wonder if God is preparing me. I'm not ready, I never will be.

We sit in the examination room at Dr. Amy's office. Doni and I are holding hands, hanging on to each other for dear life. I am being attacked with my continual feeling of impending doom and I believe Doni knows what's coming also. Dr. Amy comes in and for the first time in my life I want to run away from her. I see her as the enemy; she has the power of Doni's life in her words.

The impending doom indeed hits like a ton of bricks. The cancer is spreading rampantly now. The spots in Doni's lungs have more than doubled and three more ribs have been eaten completely away. The cancer has also eaten the second hip bone and the spine has been attacked viciously both top and bottom. The cancer has almost certainly attacked the brain although no scans were done to confirm it.

As hard as I try the tears still escape. Doni squeezes my hand and I see that he's at peace with the news. He knew already, I know he did! Doni thanks the doctor and hugs her neck. I hug her neck too and see tears in her eyes too. She whispers that she'll call me later but I already know what she's going to tell me, our time is short, horribly short!

As we walk out I take Doni's hand and he squeezes it. There are no words said on the drive home, not one. What can words offer when your hearts are breaking? We sit holding hands caught up in the fact that we're together, for now.

Doni insists that I go back to work the following day and there is a huge argument about it. "I'm not going to die for a while" he tells me and then feels bad that he'd said it. I don't want to leave him, our time has been shortened but I cave in and return to work. I've arranged for people to check in on Doni during the day which gives me a little peace of mind, very little!

Chapter 22

My heart is anxious for the call from Dr. Amy and her first words to me are "I'm so sorry Dani". She's such a sweetie; she's been so good to us and good FOR us! She tells me that Doni has at the most two more months if he's lucky. My breath stops, my heart stops and my world starts spiraling. Dr. Amy tells me that our priority now is keeping Doni as pain free as possible and drugs will be available with no questions asked.

I am also told that Hospice needs to be called in, no delaying it this time. I thank her for her kindness and tell her I'll keep in touch. I hang up the phone, put my head in my hands and let my heart fall apart.

I have to tell the family. I call my son Jeremy first, my sister Kathi next and then my mom. I've asked Kathi to call my other sister. Every phone call renews my tears. Why shouldn't it? I'd waited a long time for Doni but oh how he was worth the wait. I have to call his family and decide to call his youngest daughter first. Doni had already called her but had sugar coated the news of course.

My poor hubby is always putting his needs last, nothing changing here! I talk to his family and they discuss a schedule to come spend time, to say goodbye. I emphasize that there cannot be too many people here at one time because it would frustrate him and I wasn't going to allow it. I had shown everyone what I was made of at the hospital when I threatened them and they knew I would follow through even now.

Doni and I spend the evening discussing the schedule for everyone's plans when I get home from work. He's anxious about everything but I promise him it would work out. Doni's mind comes and goes now; it's like dealing with Alzheimer's. I have to write notes for him so he'll remember things. He's not allowed to use the microwave or stove so I've been making his breakfast before I leave for work and then have a sandwich ready for his lunch or have a friend bring something for him to eat. I have to call Doni each time he's scheduled to take his medicine or he'd forget to take it. I want to stay home but Doni still insists I go to work and as usual he wins the argument.

I've fixed dinner and he gets really quiet while I take the dishes away. I sit back down and he asks me to go over the funeral arrangements with him. "Take over God" I say," I'm out of here". I tell him that his DVD is almost done but he doesn't remember anything about it so I explain it to him, again. We discuss the songs and he beams with pride that our son Jeremy will be presiding. He asks who the pallbearers are and I rattle off the names. He thanks me for not putting any of the family on the list. He sits quietly for a minute as he's thinking then asks how many pallbearers there are. "Six", I reply.

He gives me one of his looks and informs me that he wants more. I explain to him that there are only six handles on the casket so there can't be more. He's feigning a child having a temper tantrum, looks down and points to his stomach (at this time he's over 300 pounds) and laughs, "Dani, I need at least eight" he tells me. We both break out laughing. How could I not love this man?

The discussion continues and he's satisfied with all the arrangements until he asks where he'll be buried. I tell him that he'll be buried by his first wife, there was already a plot purchased for him there. "No" he tells me, "I have to be buried with you!" He informs me that in the morning I am to make arrangements to get Linda's body exhumed and moved so he can be buried by me. I explain to him again that I'm donating my body to science and then will be cremated. My ashes, I explained can be buried with him and my name can be carved on his headstone so we'll be together.

Doni argues his thoughts one last time with me and once again I tell him what will take place emphasizing my promise to be buried with him. This latest attempt to explain things satisfies him…for now.

Chapter 23

E ven best made plans go wrong and usually to us. Almost all of Doni's family shows up in spite of being told not to come at once. Doni is happy to see everyone but it upsets him more. He can't handle the "busyness" they bring but he tries so hard to deal with it. He wants to see everyone before he dies, just not everyone at once! We find ourselves determined to just deal with what's happened, there isn't time left to change it now but it greatly tests Doni's ability for patience (and mine too if the truth is told).

Doni's oldest daughter and sister come later to spend a few days with us. This proves to be a healing time for the four of us in our relationships and everything is good until Doni's brain loses it again.

They get to witness Doni's verbal abuse and he's confused, calling them by the wrong names. The worst episode for Doni comes when he calls me Linda (his first wife's name that had died from cancer). It hadn't upset me in the least but Doni had looked at me through the eyes of a 2-year old and an-nounces "I've done something wrong haven't I?" The tears are unpreventable in loving this little boy being shown. I have to ask for the millionth time, how many times can a heart break and keep beating?

When Doni's son arrives he is jobless and fighting with his girl-friend so he has no intention of leaving. After two weeks I've had enough and call his sister to interfere. Doni's son learns his sister is coming and plans a hasty retreat. Before he leaves he asks Doni for a clock that belonged to Doni's grandmother. Our answer is no, telling him that there were plans for the clock. The subject was dropped or so we thought. Doni's son leaves the next morning and we have one night without company, such a welcome relief. Doni is of good mind and the night is perfect and relaxing.

Doni's daughter and son-in-law come last but Doni is having more problems and we end up with another trip to Dr. Amy. Doni's pain medication dosage is increased again and trying to keep track of everything he takes is proving impossible. Medication for the blood clots, the immune therapy drug, the pain patches, the oxycontin, acid reflex pills for side effects of the immune therapy drug, oxycodone, anti-inflammatory patches, Aleve for the cancer fevers.

The list is unbelievably long and between Doni's daughter and me we still have difficulty keeping it all straight. Doni is waver-ing between wanting to live and giving up. Doni tells me to call the cancer doctor in Salt Lake and get him a new immune therapy drug.

I make the call and the doctor is reluctant but I insist that he give us a new drug. "Don't mess with this crazy woman" I'm thinking; "I'm at the point I would drive the three hours to Salt Lake and slap you senseless!" "In fact, at this moment I could really use a punching bag, do you want to volunteer?" I want to say. The doctor finally concedes and tells me he'll get the insurance liaison started on contacting our insurance company.

Doni is declining rapidly and I call my boss to tell him I wouldn't be back to work. The call upsets Doni but this time I won't take no for an answer. Doni's daughter helps me convince Doni to call Hospice and he agrees. Our first nurse shows up and is this ever a shocker!

Standing at our door is our granddaughter's great-aunt (our precious little girl we can't see until she turns 18). Later Doni and I agree that maybe this was God's work at hand and the aunt would see the truth about us and help change the situation with Morgan's grandparents.

Hospice provides different nurses and they're all wonderful with Doni. They prove to be patient and willing to help us administer all the drugs necessary. The nurses make several visits a day and they are always just a phone call away.

In Hospice Doni has a new audience for his story telling and they listen diligently. Together the nurses, Doni and I spend many hours laughing and Doni loves the attention. The nurses spare nothing with making Doni happy and relaxed. As each visit ends I walk the nurse outside so I can get the facts about his condition and they're trying to prepare me for his death. Although I don't want this information, as usual it's necessary to help me deal with the situation and to plan ahead. Yes, the planner still needs to plan.

Chapter 24

Doni and I are sitting at the table, we have a night to ourselves and he tells me I need to go to the funeral home and make the arrangements for his funeral. My heart stops cold but I hear myself tell him that I would make the call. I take the phone to another room and call the funeral home before I chicken out and make arrangements for the following morning. I ask Doni's daughter if she'd go with me and she says she will.

Both of the coroners are wonderful people, I had met them through a friend of mine, an employee of theirs in dispatch who had for year's handfed my baby birds for me. Over the course of time I'd met many of her co-workers and Doni knew several of them from when his wife Linda had died.

I had grown tired of my job and had decided I wanted to start a bird store. I'd invested a lot of time and money and was getting close to my dream when Doni became sick. It had taken a long time but he was finally diagnosed with Lyme's disease. I had hired a woman to hand feed my babies and we became friends instantly. She worked at the ambulance dispatch run through the funeral home and I had to walk through a line of caskets when delivering or picking up my babies. I inherited her easiness around death and when she went to Salt Lake with me once to pick up some birds the first thing taken off each plane (different planes) were caskets. I turned to her both times and matter-of-factly stated " It could only happen with you here!" and we'd laughed our heads off. Doni had gotten jealous of my time with the birds and had once asked if I'd like him better if he had feathers. Having grown tired of the jealousy I had simply stated " Try it and see". The dream was put off but my " kids" stayed.

The meeting at the funeral home went smoothly and I thought I handled myself well. Each decision made put me one step closer to being out the door and it couldn't come fast enough for me. Friendship and kindness only go so far in a funeral home. There were no problems until discussion on the headstone. I told the coroner there was no room for a headstone between Linda's and the next headstone. We agree to meet at the cemetery and look things over and indeed Linda's headstone was in the wrong place.

"Is she in the wrong place?" I ask the coroner and I'm thinking to myself, guess we'll find out shortly huh? I return home and Doni asks lots of questions except for the price and what the casket looked like. Doni had already threatened me he'd come back and haunt me if I spent too much on a casket. We discuss the will again and go over the titles of everything we own and discuss our finances. A friend of ours had called and offered me information on items I would have to take care of when Doni died, she'd lost her husband a few years ago so had the knowledge. Her advice had helped us get ahead of the game plan so I'd have less to worry about later.

Our wills had been made out and the kids had been told what they'd get, although they would end up wanting more. Family had come and gone except for our daughter Jaime. Jaime was struggling with an alcohol and drug addiction and we'd not seen her for some time, she'd moved to Kansas. Doni insisted that he had to call and talk to her so I dialed her phone and thankfully she answered.

Doni's face is shining and I can see he's happy to be talking to her. Finally he gets around to telling her the truth, his days are numbered, and he cries. I cry with him and I can hear Jaime crying too. "Hope!" if she is crying then there's still hope that she will change.

Doni is telling her he loves her and then he hands the phone over to me, he's found himself unable to talk from crying. I can't think of what to say so tell her I'll call and let her know what's going on then hang up. Doni takes my hand and through his tears he begs me to let her come to his funeral. I promise him I'll do whatever necessary to get her here and he relaxes. Doni had adopted both my kids after we got married and although they didn't believe it he'd always loved them and had shed millions of tears over them.

Chapter 25

Doni had announced to me one morning that "things" were different. Wanting to understand his meaning I asked him to explain but he replied that he couldn't find any words for it. In desperation to know what was going on I asked other people that had lost loved ones if they'd heard this statement. Most of them said they had and it was said a few weeks before their loved ones had actually died.

Still searching for an answer I ask Doni again after his call to Jaime if he could explain what he'd meant about feeling different but he still can't materialize it to words. Maybe this is one of God's secrets, maybe even a miracle. I find it amazing how many people have witnessed the same story and know it's no coincidence.

Doni's kids keep pushing about wanting more. Doni's son had asked for a clock and had been told no and now his daughter asks if she can take it to him. She had been in in the process of going through the family pictures and I had watched how she'd carelessly discarded any pictures that included me or my kids in them. When she asked for the clock I lost it.

"Okay God, this is that straw I've heard about!" I throw the pictures at her and stomp off to the bedroom. Objects fly off the wall as I slam the door and I burst into tears. Doni, hardly able to walk opens the bedroom door, comes in and shuts the door behind him. He sits on his walker, takes my hand and cries with me. He repeatedly tells me how sorry he is about his kids.

"Are they going to take everything of you away from me like they did you when their mom died?" I ask him between my sobs. He tells me he loves me and leaves the room. I stay for some time to gather myself up but my heart is nowhere to be found. There is no forgiveness this time God, I'm sorry but enough is enough. I finally go back out to the living room and Doni sits alone. His exhaustion is obvious and he falls asleep. I sit watching him. How can people be so cruel I say over and over? Hasn't he got enough to deal with? Why should he have to protect me at a time like this?

Doni's daughter enters the room and tells me we need to talk. "Got my back God, there may be a knife coming so watch" I whisper to myself as we go outside to talk so as not to wake Doni.

"We're really here to help" she's telling me, "We know you're under a lot of stress but we want to help!" My spine is stiffening, getting ready for the knife and it comes, she's asking if she can help fill out our insurance papers. Dear God, did she actually say that? "How stupid do you think I am?" I say. "You don't have to be that way" she replies, "We know you're going to be a rich widow".

I can't decide which hurts worse, the statement itself or the word widow. Oh God, I'm going to be a widow. Why hadn't I seen that? Didn't want to and still don't. I'm completely spent, no more trying, I want out! Running back into the house I find Doni awake and he informs me that the kids are leaving in the morning. "Good" I reply, "Not soon enough" I tell myself. They leave without even saying goodbye. Neither one of us care! The peace and quiet is back, just Doni and I, the way we like it best.

I've been off work for over a week and Doni is deteriorating fast. We both know it and our conversations become urgent. We have so much time to make up for…a lifetimes worth. Just like so many others our happiness has been cut short with that one word, cancer.

Doni has begun telling his friends goodbye. He tells each one how much he loves them and thanks them for their friendship. I am so proud of Doni and his strength to get through each conversation. I know it'll be okay soon, he's going home to be with God. I still want to go with him. He hugs each friend before they leave the house and the tenderness of his heart overwhelms them and me. There are so many things I love about him and I will miss every one of them when he leaves me.

We spend our time holding hands and exchanging stories of our lives. Doni sleeps a lot and I miss him so much during these times. "Get used to it" my mind tells me and my heart tells it to shut up. This is nothing compared to how it'll be but I'll do this. I've never loved anyone more than I love this man.

Doni wakes up, takes my hand, and looks at me and smiles. "Thank you" he says. "What do you mean" I reply. "For taking such good care of me, for dealing with everything, for being part of my life, for loving me!" he says. Okay, promise broken. The dam of tears breaks open and I hold him in my arms crying. "I don't want to lose you" I get out between sobs. Doni is crying too and we take the time to cry out our pain of losing each other. We again sit holding hands looking at each other. We have no words for a time; our hearts are on the table where they have fallen. We know now as we've always known; we were supposed to be together. Dani and Doni, how perfect!

Chapter 26

Thursday night (August 27th)

Doni's pain is really bad and he's slept most of the day. He woke up in the late afternoon and asked if we could take a ride. "Of course we can" I tell him, even if I have to carry him to the car. We take a drive around town, looking up old memories. I show him new projects around town, the ones he's missed while being sick. He tires easily and is ready to go home. He doesn't want to eat. "Its' okay honey", I know!

Friday morning (August 28th)

Doni wakes me up just before 4 AM screaming my name. I'm scared! Hospice has been warning me that Doni will suffer a horrible death and I've been begging God to let them be wrong. Doni is panicked and wants to be taken to the dining room table. I get him to his chair and he tells me we really need to talk. He takes my hand and rubs the diamond in my wedding ring. I compare the sparkle of the diamond to the sparkle in his eyes and realize the diamond doesn't come close, not at all.

"I love you" he tells me. "Yes honey, I know that and you know that I love you too" I reply. "I'm going to be leaving you" he tells me and I panic. "Now" I ask? "No" he replies, "In a few days". I'm speechless but thankful that it's not today. "Don't let my kids screw you" he tells me for the hundredth time. He makes me go over the will again and finally asks "Are you sure you get everything?"

"Everything is taken care of" I tell him. Doni asks several questions and finally breathes a sigh of relief but gets upset again realizing he's not told me how to take care of things around the house and attempts to give me a crash course, house repairs 101. I reassure him that I'll find help and he relaxes once again. "You know what to do when I keel over?" he asks me. He's still trying to be the jokester and I answer him "Yes dear, I call Hospice!" Looking as serious as a typical 2-year old he scorns me "No Dani, you're supposed to call 9-1-1". We both laugh but I explain to him about why Hospice is called just to calm his mind. He's appeased with my answer and he tells me he's tired and asks me to take him back to his recliner. He immediately falls asleep.

How can anyone be so amazing I wonder, especially in a time like this? I'd been told stories from other cancer families about their loved ones having the same attitude but I'd also heard horror stories of patients who weren't so fortunate. Blessings are everywhere; we've seen so many of them through all of this. "Thank you God" I say now.

I watch Doni and finally put my head down to pray "God, please keep me strong for Doni, let my faith grow and teach me the lessons I need for later" then continue "And please God let Doni die easily, let him find peace even though it means my sorrow". Doni's done so much for me over the years and I tell God that he deserves to go to heaven for being crazy enough to marry me and stay with me all these years. Yes, heaven is what he deserves, I'll own up to that!

Saturday (August 29th)

I call my son Jeremy and ask him if he can stay with Doni so I can go to the store. Jeremy is given all the phone numbers and instructions to call me with any change. When I return I find Doni and Jeremy sitting at the dining room table talking. They're engrossed in their conversation so I excuse myself and let them have some time together, this could be the last. Doni needs to go to the bathroom and my son helps him get up from the table and gets his walker for him before he leaves to go home. Doni still wants privacy so he shuts the door although I stand guard outside.

"Are you okay" I ask after some time. "Yes" he replies. The time gets longer and longer but he answers each time I ask if he's okay. I finally suspect something is wrong and I open the door to find the 2-year old Doni grinning back at me, unbelievably naked! My heart hits the ground but I smile at him and tell him we need to get him dressed. I am shocked as to how he could be naked because he's been unable to dress or undress himself for a long time. Just another of life's mysteries I assume. I'll store this memory for later I tell myself. My precious little boy, my husband, my best friend!

Doni tries to eat but he's too tired. I take him back to his chair and sleep takes hold once more. I get a folding chair and sit beside him holding his hand. I have to memorize his face, pictures won't be enough. I watch his chest. I put my hand to his heart and tell him how much I love him and how much I will miss him when he's gone. I ask him if he'll meet me at Heaven's gate when it's my time to go and then beg God for the same.

I had told Doni I wanted to go with him when he left but he told me it wasn't to be, he knew it would be quite a while till I got to come. I had asked Doni how he knew that and he grinned at me and said "God and I both know what a perfectionist you are with your house and it's going to take the both of us a long time to get it done...right" he'd added. I had laughed but knew that Doni had gotten one more shot in." Good for you honey" I think.

My arm gets tired and so has my mind. I get up and kiss him and go to the computer room. I go over the pictures for Doni's DVD and tell myself the stories that go to each one. How many times had we laughed I wonder? How many tears have we shed? Doni and I had made a promise to never go to bed angry and thankfully we'd kept that promise but we'd really had few fights throughout our marriage. I had waited forever to find love but I'd waited to receive the very best of it. I had never thought I deserved Doni but God gave him to me anyway, in spite of me being me. "Isn't God merciful and loving?" I ask myself now. "Yes Scarlet, take that one!"

Chapter 27

Saturday afternoon

Doni is agitated. He won't wake up but keeps making the same movements over and over. I call Hospice and the nurse comes. She watches for a time and thinks he wants his handkerchief. Doni had always carried one in his front pocket. She talks to him and gives him his handkerchief but he's not deterred. He keeps up the movements. The nurse explains to me that cancer patients do this a lot, some type of movement they've done habitually during their lifetime.

A smoker she explains will make the gestures of getting a cigarette and lighting it and could make the motions of actually smoking. The nurse keeps talking to Doni as I try to figure out what he's doing when the light bulb finally comes on. Doni's always been a welder; he's lighting the welding rod in his stinger and getting ready to weld. How many mysterious marvels can cancer patients bring to our lives I ask as I sit in awe?

Speechless for a moment I watch Doni's persistence in getting the job done. The nurse begins talking to him, telling him what a good job he's doing. As she continues talking she tells him that it looked like he was about finished and then when he finally stops she praises him for a job well done. What did I just witness? My mind is still soaking it in when his eyes open. He's smiling from ear to ear but he's looking past my shoulder.

His smile gets bigger if that's possible.

He doesn't hear my voice. Whatever is there is occupying all of him. "His angel" I say excitedly, "He's seeing his angel!" Another of Gods gifts I think as Doni's eyes close again and he's restful. The work is done for Doni and his heart must surely be at peace now.

The Hospice nurse and I go outside to talk. My time with Doni has been shortened to not weeks but just days. The emptiness is already setting in. The nurse tells me that Doni will completely quit eating and drinking but that it is part of the death process. Helping Doni is first and foremost now; I have to make this transition as easy as I can for him. "Hear that God?" I whisper. "Are you as surprised as I am?" I finish. I realize again that Doni has inherited his strength to me. His love still continues to shine, to fill me, to inspire me.

The nurse leaves and I go inside and try to eat something. I sit in Doni's chair at the dining room table and watch him sleeping. I think about all the things that have changed since we found out about his cancer. I know that nothing has been the same, nor will they ever be again.

Doni was the one that had kept things positive through our lives, much like my grandmother. I found it ridiculous at times that people could be so "up"!

I had called my grandmother in Missouri once to check up on her and she had informed me that her mailman had been attacked by several Rottweiler's and may not survive. Not in the mood for her positivity I had challenged her to find something positive out of the situation and she excitedly answered. "Oh my, you should see my new mailman!" I was shocked but my laughter came before I could contain it. Doni had found it hilarious and had chastised me to "lighten up a little". Chalk another one up for Doni, one for Grandma too!

Chapter 28

The first set of papers we had received from the cancer clinic stated that hope is 90% of the treatment for cancer. Websites we had looked at also said the same; the need for hope is foremost. People that have never experienced cancer can't begin to imagine finding hope through cancer; cancer patients and their families can't imagine life without it, they cling to it. Cancer brings out the best and worst of people and shows us what little control we have over our lives. Cancer is a cleanser of souls and makes us face our past transgressions. Cancer also opens our eyes to truths we didn't want to face and changes people, forever!

Doni is still sleeping. My mind is tired from all the thinking so I go back to the computer. This time I play games, anything it takes to make me escape the truth if just for a while. The fact is I'm tired of watching Doni die. I want it over with now, for both of us. Guilt hits me with the thought and I ask God to strike me with lightening for even thinking such a thing. How could I possibly feel this way?

The reality is that the majority of people feel this near the end, if they're honest enough to admit it. I don't want Doni to die and I don't want to live without him. The truth is that Doni isn't living now. Sitting in a chair sleeping; being in horrible constant pain is a living death. I don't know what I want, is mercy what I'm asking for?

Saturday night

I'm restless. Sleep is out of reach. I take a chair and sit by Doni again holding his hand. I get up and walk through the house remembering a lifetime of stories. I go outside on the porch he built me, my "labor of love" I'd told him. I pray and cry and pray some more. My heart is heavy and my mind won't quit thinking. I go back in and kiss Doni on the top of his head, his lips have become unresponsive and the morphine leaks from his mouth. I kiss his head once more and this time he cries out in pain. "God, can't I even kiss him anymore" I cry out.

I'm mad and hurt and lost.

I sit back in my chair and tell him how much I love him and tell him stories that mean the most to me. I get up and go sit in Doni's chair at the dining room table and put my head in my hands and cry. I know Doni can probably hear me but I can't control them. Doni is on his journey home and my tears can only be a sign to him of how much I truly love him. I'm not ashamed of my tears; Doni's earned every one of them. I cry even harder as the sadness sets in that this love will be gone. How many times can a heart be broken and still work I ask myself for the millionth time? I know I'm about to set a world record but I've lost count. Oh well, not a record people would strive to beat anyway.

Chapter 29

Sunday (August 30th)

Doni's still hanging on. He hasn't eaten or had anything to drink for 24 hours now. He's pretty much in a coma. I go take my shower and I have to touch everything he last touched; and remember. I hold his razor, brush my hand against the medicine cabinet, and touch the support handle to the shower. I'm walking memory lane although he's still here; barely!

I've arranged for my sister Kathi to come after Church and sit with Doni while I feed my birds. I'm afraid to leave him alone; I have to be there to hold him when he leaves.

I remember walking into a pet store and telling Doni there was a sick bird in the store. "How do you know that" he'd asked." I can hear it" I told him.

I was right. The woman from the store had tried to hand feed the baby bird not knowing anything about the process. The little bird's lungs had been filled with formula and it was suffocating.

I begged the woman to let me take it home because I didn't want it to die alone. The woman had refused and Doni had stepped in and bought the bird for me, no questions asked. I had held the little bird until it died the next day and then Doni held me while I cried.

Doni is amazing, my knight in shining armor minus the white horse. We'd had horses but white ones were off limits to him. No matter, he'd still won me over.

Now I won't have him to comfort me I think and I cry even harder. I leave the room for a moment to try to gain composure and when I come back Doni wakes up and smiles at me. I'm happy because I know he sees me. His smile is radiating through his eyes and the look is different. "Angelic?" I ask myself. No, much more than that! I think. "Hi honey, did you wake up?" I ask him and he looks at me for a few seconds more before his eyes close and the smile fades. Sleep has overtaken him again.

My sister comes and I go to feed the birds. I'm not there long when she comes running down the stairs. "Something's wrong" she yells. I run up the stairs and Doni is visually agitated. "What's wrong honey?" I ask him. It only takes a minute to realize the answer; my sister had switched the television station to a football game. I go through the channels until I find a program about Alaska bears and he settles down instantly. My sister looks at me with shock and I tell her "He didn't like the game" as I go back downstairs to finish my chores.

When I get done with my birds I come back upstairs to finish watching the bear program with Doni and my sister. I make comments to Doni during the show, something we'd always done throughout our married life. My sister eventually leaves and Doni and I are alone. He hasn't woken up since that beautiful smile earlier. I wonder if this was my goodbye and know that it is something I will treasure in my heart, ALWAYS!

Later that evening a friend calls and tells me she can't quit thinking about Doni and I tell her he's going to die very soon. It hits her hard and she begs to come over but I won't let her. I had promised Doni that there would be no visitors to see him in this state. She's disappointed but Doni's wishes come first I tell her, I'm sorry! "Give him a kiss and tell him it's from me" she says and I promise her I will do it immediately after hanging up. I keep her promise and kiss him telling him it's from her. No sign of pain this time and I thank God for another small miracle.

Sunday night

Miraculously I've fallen asleep but wake up in a second. Doni's breathing has changed. I call Hospice and they have the nurse on duty call. It's our granddaughter's great-aunt. I put the phone where she can hear Doni's breathing and she tells me it's just part of the process, not to worry. I get the chair back out and sit beside Doni holding his hand, telling him how much I love him over and over. I put my other hand to his chest and feel his heart beating and watch his chest rise and fall. Slowly, slower, Oh God, it's not moving! After a few seconds it moves again but it felt like a lifetime. It happens again and I call Hospice.

I scream in the phone "Get here now" and hang up. It hits me that I didn't tell them who I was but surely they would know since I'd just called twenty minutes ago. The nurse on duty only lives a few streets away I know so it won't take long for her to get here. I continue to hold Doni's hand; my other hand placed on his chest.

When the next breath is slow in coming I call out his name. Doni takes another breath and then a longer pause, one more breath and another long pause. I call his name again and he takes a third breath. I see headlights pull in the driveway. One more breath and I wait. There isn't another one, nothing! The nurse comes to the door and I scream at her to come in. Doni still hasn't taken a breath and I look at the nurse with desperation.

"I think he's gone" I say in shock to her. She checks for a pulse and finds none. "He's gone" she tells me. "He's really gone?" I ask her and I begin to cry.

Chapter 30

It's just after midnight which makes it August 31st, 2009. I'm listening to the nurse who's trying to console me, I try to pay attention but I'm thinking how it had ended just like I'd asked God. We were alone, just the two of us and he had gone peacefully. No struggling, no suffocation, just one final breath and Doni was gone. "Thank you God for making it easy for him" I say through my tears.

I make phone calls which I don't remember making. My son told me that when he answered his phone I merely told him that his Dad was in heaven. That's good I think. The nurse stays with me, she makes calls too. She waits till my family arrives before having the coroner come so they can have time alone with Doni and me. I am numb in knowing that Doni has really died.

I look again at Doni and see he's so very white; the life had drained quickly leaving only his shell. One of Doni's major concerns had been that he would have that painful "cancer look" we'd seen on too many faces of our friends who'd died from cancer. When the coroner arrives I am in bad shape. I can't decide if I'm still sane or if I should go with the flow of being crazy. My first concern is telling the coroner over and over how white Doni is and how it has to be changed. "I don't want him white" I keep repeating like a crazy person. My thought changes quickly and I see who has come with the coroner. There are only two employees of the ambulance; both women and I ask the coroner where his help is. He doesn't understand my question and I take him to see Doni who is over 300 pounds. The coroner calls for more help and then takes me aside to say he doesn't think Doni will fit in the coffin I'd ordered. Still playing jokes on me Doni? Wonderful I tell myself! I think I'll decide on the choice of being crazy, it'll be much easier.

The nurse calls me to the front door where a sheriff stands. He'd seen the ambulance and asked if he could help in any way. I tell him that my husband had just passed away and he is embarrassed that he's interrupted. He apologizes several times although I tell him that it was fine; it made me feel good that he'd stopped to check.

The extra help arrives and the coroner tells me we can have a few minutes alone with Doni before they take him. What am I supposed to say? Words have escaped me so I touch my hand to his cheek. How many times had he done that to me? I told Doni that I would never tell him goodbye but I truly don't remember what I said at that moment or if I'd said anything at all. I didn't care, Doni was gone and that's all I could feel at the moment.

The coroner comes back in and tells me they're going to take Doni's body. Our poor dog goes nuts barking. Ty was never one to bark until the minute Doni died and he'd barked and barked then flopped on the floor and hadn't moved since. He gets up now and follows the stretcher with Doni's body outside and the whole time he's barking. Once they have Doni in the vehicle and the doors shut Ty returns to his spot in the house and flops back down on the floor. He's broken, just like me.

I had gone to Missouri with my sister Kathi when our Dad had his stroke. I spoke with Doni continuously; of course the modern age of cell phones was upon us. I remember a conversation when Doni had asked me if I could guess what he'd found in our laundry. After several wrong guesses he'd told me he'd found a baby seal. At first I thought someone had moved my stuffed one but Doni informed me it was very much alive.

After challenging Doni as to his state of sobriety he'd told me it was a puppy that our daughter Jaime had brought home. He did in fact look like a baby seal, all white with a black nose and eyes. He turned out to be a miniature American Eskimo dog; the whole litter had been abandoned around town. The poor thing was scared of his shadow and if you just raised your voice to him he would tremble and pee down his leg. By the time I got home the dog had won over the household and was a permanent fixture. Doni's dog Patch tolerated him so I had no vote here, like it would have mattered. Doni wasn't the only one with a tender heart when it came to animals!

The nurse says she's leaving, hugs my neck and tells me how sorry she is about Doni. My sister is exhausted so I convince her to go home. My son stays; he doesn't want to leave me alone. We talk, shed tears and some laughter as we share some of our memories. Finally I tell him that he needs to go home. I need time alone; I need time to cry, to think and to talk to God.

My son leaves and I can feel the emptiness of the house, something I had never imagined. Exhaustion takes over and I sit in my recliner and unbelievably fall asleep. I had made the recliner my bed a long time ago.

I wake up seeing Doni's empty chair and then see Ty. The poor dog hasn't moved an inch. I call him and finally he jumps in my lap but he doesn't stay long. He wants to "mourn" in his own way. I don't want to move or to take another breath for that matter. I know there is much to do because people will be coming and there are plans to be made. Where's the master planner now? She's too tired and too broken I think, just leave her alone!

As I sit in the quiet I hear Doni's chair in the dining room move. I sit up to look and hear it squeak like it did when he'd sit down in it. I hear Doni's watch scratching the table (there's a scratch mark in the table from the many times Doni had done this) and then I hear him clear his throat as he had every morning for months. I'm not hearing things because I know I'm awake. Doni is checking on me and I think "How cool is this?"

Chapter 31

I call Doni's friend from work, a man that had worked for Doni in Oregon and now worked with me at the plant, he also lives down the street. I tell him that Doni has passed away and ask if he'd inform people at work with an email, I have enough calls to deal with. Eventually I call the plant and tell the shift supervisor that Doni had died and to let my boss know I would call him when I knew something. The day has begun, my new life has too. Sad, unwilling but it's mine!

I decide to go get my shower. I end up putting my head against the shower wall and bawling; I believe my tears are creating more water than the shower. Maybe I can set another record? Who cares! Not me!

After getting dressed I sit down in Doni's chair at the dining room table. I need to make a list of what has to be done. There are calls to make, flowers to purchase and then my mind goes blank. I can't fall apart now I tell myself, there's too much to do.

The coroner calls and tells me the coffin is okay, another miracle received through all this. I wish now I'd written them all down and wonder just how many pages it would take to list them all. I think back over all the things that had strengthened us and I vow to Doni that I will make him proud of me. I tell God the same thing.

My son arrives and he joins in helping me make the list of things that need to be done. Two heads are better than one don't they say, too bad mine has gone empty, like my heart.

It's Monday, the funeral will be on Friday. Doni insisted that his funeral be at my Church. His wife Linda's funeral had been at the same building but it had been an Assembly of God Church at that time. This was an important issue to Doni but I told him that the building would never hold everyone that would show up for his funeral. He'd responded by telling me matter-of-factly "Let them stand!"

My son is asking what I want to be presented in Doni's eulogy. I remember the look on Doni's face when I had told him Jeremy would be presiding, he'd been so proud! Doni had loved me so much during our lives together and just days before he'd died he had made me promise him that I'd be okay. I hadn't meant to lie but today I question my answer, I'm not so sure! Coming back to the present I tell my son the story about how our roles had reversed as to what the judge had told us when we got married. I also tell Jeremy about a clock that Doni had bought me that couldn't ever keep time. Doni had announced later down the road that the clock had been a perfect gift because like me it was always "a little off". I had laughed then and I have to laugh now!

The doorbell rings and the first flowers are delivered. Doni had loved flowers and plants with a passion. I killed them; I only had to look at them and they croaked. No green thumb here! Doni on the other hand had planted something to fill empty spots in the yard, didn't matter what and almost everything grew. Of course there was no rhyme or reason to our landscaping but Doni was happy. Friends start trickling in and the first of the six tons of food we end up with starts showing up.

Stories get told about Doni and people tell me how much he'd meant to them. My heart swells with pride as I ask Doni "You thought I was the only one your life touched, are you listening to all this?"

I finally make contact with my friend that had sent Doni the kiss and let her know that Doni was gone. Doni was well loved and respected; he'd always been straight forward with his beliefs and views and had been admired for it. A straight shooter they said; would they still think that if they heard some of the hunting stories he'd told me in secret?

Chapter 32

The first thing I had done the morning Doni died was to call a neighbor and ask if she could send help to remove Doni's recliner, looking at it was proving unbearable. I look at the empty spot now and the cat lies where the chair had been. She's mourning too! The dog still lies where he had dropped earlier that morning and hasn't moved.

My grandson Bailey has just arrived and the dog must hear him. Ty is up and at the door looking for him. Bailey can't walk for the dog being all over him. I'm happy to see my boy, happier to see that Ty has come back to life. Bailey has been one of our greatest blessings over the years. Doni had learned how to "power up" with the power rangers, learned how to share "his toys" (yes, I'm talking about Doni's) along with receiving hundreds of other lessons, the most important being patience.

The one Christmas we had got to see our grand-daughter before she had been taken away found Bailey somewhat jealous. Doni, trying to resolve the situation tells Bailey he needs help in putting one of Morgan's toys together. Doni had handed the instructions to Bailey, telling him to read off the instructions and Doni would put it together. Bailey had taken the paper and looked at it, looked back at papa and then back to the paper. After several repetitions of this Doni asked Bailey, "What do the instructions say?" to which Bailey promptly replied "Do it right!" I thought Doni and I would both choke to death from laughing.

Bailey hugs my neck when he walks in the room and tells me he loves me. I ask him to take the dog out and play with him because he was sad; the truth was that I didn't want Bailey to hear the "adult talk" that was taking place. When it comes time for Bailey to leave a little later the dog watches him get in the car and flops back on the floor. I can't take the pain from watching it and call Baileys grandparents later that night to ask if Bailey could take the dog. Thank God they agree.

The next day Bailey arrives to take Ty and the dog comes to life and runs to the door. Bailey plays with the dog as we pack up all Ty's belongings and put them in the trunk of their car. Watching Bailey get in the car the dog falls to the pavement devastated. Bailey tells Ty to come and the dog just looks at him. Bailey calls a second time and Ty stands up unsure of what's going on. The third time Bailey calls he slaps his hands on his legs as he tells Ty "Come on". Ty jumps in the car and never looks back; he's busy licking the poor kid to death. They leave and my son puts his arm around me and asks if I'm okay.

How can I not be happy for him, for both of them? They have each other now, new best buds! We head back to the house; I turn around and look at the empty driveway. "Bet he never calls or writes" I tell my son and we go inside the house.

Chapter 33

The coroner calls and tells me I can come see Doni. I want to pass out but know I have to do this, just get it over with. I take my son and sister with me, I can't go alone. I say a little prayer before we enter the funeral home.

"He's not white" I hear myself say. No sign of that cancer look Doni had so dreaded. He honestly looks like he's sleeping peacefully, just one more miracle for the list! I hug the coroner and tell him that Doni would be so pleased with how he looks. The casket is beautiful and I thank God the material isn't white inside.

Doni hated white because "it stains too fast" he'd told me. "You see this honey?" I ask him. I had remembered! I stand and marvel at how peaceful Doni looks. I brush his cheek with my hand and tell him again how much I love him. Now after all these years I must add the words "and miss you". I tell Doni I have to leave and take care of other business but that I'd see him later.

Never goodbye! Never!

Unbelievably I look around as we exit the room for any signs of Doni paying good on his promise to haunt me if I paid too much for his casket. "Guess I finally got one over on you, right honey?" I say as a shiver runs down my spine.

I finish paying for everything and the coroner goes over details of the funeral with my son. Arrangements are made for the DVD, the viewing and for the funeral service. We leave, next stop is flowers. I had never cared for red flowers, Doni didn't like white (figure that one out) so we'd finally agreed on yellow. Doni's first gift to me had been yellow roses and to this day they hold a special place in my heart. I had known with receiving those first flowers that we were going to be together for the rest of our lives. Man was this ever a short forever I think.

My sister, son and I pick out flowers for the funeral, pay for them and head to the Mexican restaurant to plan a luncheon. Oh how Doni and I had loved this restaurant. We had become friends with the owners who were absolutely precious people. I wanted to have a luncheon after the service for family and special friends. Doni would have loved it! The three of us decide to have lunch while we're there and it hits me that this is my first meal out since Doni had died. My sister and son have to carry on the conversations, my heart is elsewhere.

Home again, new meaning to the word. It doesn't have the same ring to it, nor does it have the comfortable feeling either. How many other things have changed I ask myself. Lots of people come to visit over the next few days, more food gets delivered. Too bad I'm not the least bit hungry! Cancer had taken away Doni's appetite and now it's stolen mine. Long arms huh? Big claws I decide. Am I handling this as well as others that have gone through this? I can only hope to show a small portion of the dignity Doni had showed.

Cancer may have taken my hubby but I wasn't going to allow it to steal my soul...hopefully! I say a quick prayer for everyone cancer has affected, sending my sympathy to all whether they win or lose the fight. Its hell either way I've decided. Why is it that we can see the courage in others and overlook our own?

Another friend from work shows up with more money. Doni had told me to be charitable before he died so I decide to divide the money between two institutions that had helped us through this long ordeal as well as buying Doni's headstone. The first place was of course Hospice, no surprise there. The second is a local organization called Cowboys against Cancer who helps people with cancer by giving them money to help with traveling expenses. We have no local facility for cancer treatment and have to travel to Salt Lake City, Utah for help. Doni and I had received a check for $2500 and we had cried like babies. Strangers helping strangers!

When Doni's wife Linda had died he had taken the money collected at work to buy her headstone. Doni had said that in doing this he could always see the love from friends when he visited Linda's grave. I wanted to feel that same love so continued a tradition that Doni had started. "Don't tell me there isn't good in this world", I've seen it firsthand.

The viewing is set for Thursday night. My family goes early. I was surprised by all the flowers. "Oh Doni do you know how much you were loved?" I say to him. Sitting by the casket is an arrangement I'd had made to symbolize the first flowers Doni had given me, yellow roses. This will be my last physical present to my husband; the circle has been completed now. How short our time had turned out to be but we'd filled it to the brim. No regrets we'd told each other several times. Our love had grown and matured while our lives had bonded and all was good!

Chapter 34

I had already watched the DVD for Doni so I would be prepared. There are over two hundred people who come to pay their respects. Many of the people share more stories of Doni; all of them treasured pieces of my hubby's life. My grandson Bailey comes but he doesn't want to see papa. I tell him that's okay that papa understood. How difficult funerals must be for children, they don't understand the finality in it.

My daughter Jaime has come and she sees Bailey. She's been warned not to cause any scenes; she had abandoned him and must stay away from him. She leaves so she can cry.

I hadn't wanted her to come but Doni had made me promise and I always keep my promises to him. Bailey's grandparents (who have custody of him) go outside and fear takes hold of me. I'm already numb from the viewing for Doni but this new situation makes me think I'll pass out for sure. When I go outside to see what is going on I find the three of them hugging. Immediately I know this is why Doni had insisted Jaime had to be at his funeral. The three of them walk back into the funeral home holding hands and Jaime is introduced to Bailey. Not as his mother but as my daughter and she hugs Bailey's neck.

Chalk up another miracle won't you God, one that Doni had helped on.

Doni's family had showed up but only a couple of them go inside to pay their respects. Doni would be embarrassed, I'm embarrassed too. I hope God doesn't allow him to see this. Aside from Doni's family the evening goes well and I'm relieved to have it over. I'm tired and I want to go home. I'm filled with so many emotions but don't want to deal with any of them. I know sleep won't come tonight but I want to be alone. I have a lifetime of memories to go over.

I arrive at the Church the next morning for the funeral; I go early so I can visit with Doni before people start showing up. There are even more flowers today and Doni is still sleeping peacefully. How long has it been since he could lie down I wonder. Recliners have been our beds for so long. Sleep well my love, you deserve it!

People start to arrive and I go to meet them. I have decided to continue what Doni started and I hug everyone that enters the Church. I thank each person that comes and tell them that Doni would be pleased. Bailey arrives and takes my hand and holds it when I'm not hugging people. How proud Doni would be of Bailey today, he was always proud of him anyway. "I won't let go" Bailey tells me. I stand in awe of this child with the beautiful heart, this little boy that has brought so much happiness to our lives. The Church is full and I remember Doni telling me "Let them stand". They're going to have to I tell him now.

My friend from the funeral home comes and tells me they need to close the casket and start the service. I take Bailey to his grandmother sitting towards the back so he won't have to view Doni's body. Bailey grabs my hand in a death grip and tells me "I'm not leaving you Granny!" I exchange looks with Bailey's grandmother and we both have immense pride for him written on our faces.

Bailey and I turn to go take that long walk to the front but when I get to the aisle I freeze. I can't move, can't do this, no way! Two of my friend's see what's happening (as does a lot of the people in attendance) and they come to me. I let go of Bailey's hand and grab them around their necks for a lifeline. "I can't do this" I tell them. "I won't get to see his face anymore and I won't see those beautiful eyes" and through a multitude of tears I cry to them "He can't touch my cheek, I won't have the strength from his touch anymore".

They're crying, I'm crying and over and over I keep telling them "I can't do this, don't make me do this!" I feel Bailey take my hand and he squeezes it just like Doni had done! I stop cold in my tracks and look at him when he says "Its okay, I'm here!" I'm stunned at the words and look into Baileys eyes to see the same sparkle I'd seen in Doni's and I wonder how I could have ever missed it. I can feel the strength in his hand just the same as I had felt in Doni's. Is this all new? Here stands a young man as beautiful and tender as the man I had just lost and I realize this was to be my most memorable miracle ever.

Doni was standing there in the form of this child but it wasn't Doni. "God, you're such a better planner than I ever could be,

141

thank you!" I tell Him. Bailey and I smile at each other, squeeze each other's hands and although we can hear the sobbing of people we walk hand in hand to the front of the Church. "The widows walk" I think to myself.

I sit Bailey down in the front pew and go to the casket with my son Jeremy and daughter Jaime. I stand to the side so they have time to say their goodbyes. No one knows that I am committed to never use the word myself.

It's my turn, my final look. I won't cry I tell Doni though my tears are falling. "No regrets remember?" I say to him. I put one hand on his heart and hold his hand with the other, just as I had done when he left me and I promise him again; "I'll love you forever!" I stand there as the funeral home attendants come. I could never have imagined myself in this position.

Nine months flash through my mind as I stand at Doni's side. Cancer, terminal, your time is limited, he's gone! The words run through my head and then I hear Doni begging me "Promise me you'll be okay!" I shed more tears at this thought but promise him once again "Yes honey, someday I'll be okay again!" I turn to leave but my heart makes me turn back, lean over the casket and I whisper, "Play nice with the angel's honey!"

THE MIRACLE OF CANCER...

I'm sure by now you've wondered about the title of the book and asked yourselves if I am indeed crazy (mentioned several times throughout the book and still being debated).

If you look up the word miracle in the Webster's dictionary it is defined as:

Definition # 1

An extraordinary event manifesting divine intervention in human affairs

Manifest = readily perceived by the senses, especially the sight.

Divine = direct from God

Intervene = coming between points of time or events

> Doni's diagnosis of cancer allowed us both to see that God indeed has a plan for us, both here on earth and again in Heaven. Doni and I were both awarded "glimpses of God's eternal love" through this journey.

Definition # 2

An extremely outstanding or unusual event, thing or accomplishment

Doni's death produced accomplishments for both of us.

Loving EACH OTHER unselfishly to the end and witnessing the growth of our belief in God is what accomplished our decision to not let cancer destroy us.

MY biggest accomplishment was receiving all the blessings Doni left behind in my heart and seeing God's lessons through Doni's life.
As for Doni, he accomplished his job in teaching me about life and love and is now rewarded for a job well done.

Definition # 3

A divinely natural phenomenon experienced humanly as the fulfillment of spiritual law

Divine = direct from God

Natural = based on an inherent sense of right and wrong

Phenomenon= observable occurrences

Spiritual law = relating to, consisting of or affecting the spirits rule of conduct enforced by a controlling authority

God wrote Doni's story and with it came the faith Doni and I needed to know that God was right in using us to tell it.

Some would argue that the only miracle of cancer would be the "survival" of the cancer patient, family members or all of the above.

Others would like to suggest that "love" could define this miracle.

If you will, you could say that any of the miracles contained in this book could be the miracle, which of course they are miracles BUT...

My definition of a miracle:

A validation of the belief in God's great love...

And to me that was DONI!
God had used Doni for a miracle in my life.

SUMMARY:

Did Doni and I want this miracle? We didn't want the journey but it was our decision to allow God's love to take over to help us get through it. All that was needed from us was to open our hearts to God and with that; our last nine months together were the most cherished of our time together.

I can honestly tell you that I struggled for sixteen months after I lost Doni and went through a journey of hell called grief. Hopefully I will be able to write about this also because it is indeed the "roller coaster ride" of a lifetime no one wants to ride. The events that occurred through this journey of grief were some of the most unbelievable and challenging of my life, AND YES, the miracles were very abundant through this journey too!

At this time I would like to send prayers to cancer patients and their families. Remember that your best defense is hope and that God is the creator of it! I hope that you've noticed I have never used the term "victim" because we aren't! Victims let their "attacker" cheat them of something in their lives and although Doni's life was cut short we were never cheated of our love for each other or our belief in God.

SAFELY IN HIS ARMS

I am safely in our Fathers arms
So please don't cry for me,
Your sadness will soon go away
And joy again you'll see.

I took half your heart to heaven
And left half of mine with you,
So when your tears start falling
My love will get you through.

Remember our times together
Think often of things we shared,
Remember the smiles and laughter
And how much I really cared.

The Miracle of CANCER

I am safely in our Fathers arms
And someday you will be too,
When your time on earth is over
I'll be here waiting for you.

Written by Dani Gibson
For Doni's funeral announcement

PICTURE

The following picture was a "gift of love" given by my boss, one of Doni's former employees in Oregon. There was an insistence from Larry that I wouldn't receive the picture if he couldn't get Doni's eyes right.

This was the confirmation to my thoughts that I fell in love with Doni's eyes first...the mirror to the person that captured my heart.

Although Doni told many stories during our life together, the picture told one I had never heard.

The story:

Doni and his Dad were fishing when an eagle swooped down beside them to capture a fish. Unknown to the eagle the fish was too large for the bird to carry off but the eagle wasn't deterred. Doni had told his fellow co-workers that the bird had "skipped" the fish on the surface of the water and it had been like watching a rock being skipped on the water.

The eagle had finally gotten flight and almost made it to the nearest tree when it lost grip of the fish.

This had to be Doni's biggest story of "The one that got away"!

Doni Gibson
Drawn by Larry Cundick

The following pages contain…

A preview of "The Possibilities in Grief"

A message to Doni's family

Although Doni's story in "The Miracle of Cancer" has reflections of hurt between family members I want everyone to know that love outweighs anything that might have happened and forgiveness can be found by anyone who trust's in God.

A poem about forgiveness

"The Possibilities in Grief"

I thought the hardest part of my husband's journey through cancer was watching him die slowly. As Doni's death drew closer I knew in my heart that watching his actual death would be even harder. Unfortunately neither one proved right. As a friend pointed out the hardest part of losing a loved one is taking that first breath after they've died.

I now know that this first breath is the beginning of your grief process and you will find it the most unbelievable, heart wrenching roller coaster ride that takes you to the very outskirts of hell itself.

At times you'll find yourself so numb that you can't see the ride, in other times you'll wish you could go back and just stay numb. Remember that people survive horrible encounters every day; floods, tornados, fires and yes, the loss of a loved one. The most important thing for you to know is that grief is only a temporary setback in our lives and just like in all tragedies our human spirit survives to pull us through and we find ourselves stronger and tenderer.

The process I chose to take in grieving is what I thought right for me and you must find the best choices for yourself; no one can take the journey for you. I discovered early that I learned more by talking to people that have travelled this road already. I found I was willing to hear what they had experienced during their grief but found myself using only the information that I felt I could use.

You've obviously taken that first breath…

NOW KEEP ON BREATHING!

TO DONI'S FAMILY

Messages of the heart...

There are many forms of forgiveness a person has to realize during the grief process. Just one form is finding forgiveness for personal hurt caused by others in your life. One of my biggest challenges was dealing with my feelings about Doni's family. I loved Doni with all I am and thought this should be enough to be accepted by his family members. I had never, EVER, stopped to think about their feelings in having Doni marry less than a year after losing his first wife Linda to cancer (the mother of his three kids). I realize now the hurt they must have felt, and maybe even experienced a sense of betrayal. In trying to heal myself I had to change my feeling of hurt towards Doni's family to forgiveness which meant understanding there was more than me that had been hurt.

After looking at all our hearts and the pain that has been experienced, I can only pray that

157

someday forgiveness will be shared by all of us. I hope Doni's family will allow God to one day replace their pain with the fact that Doni had found someone that loved him with all her heart. I can apologize for hurting family members because I am truly sorry but I will never apologize for loving Doni and sharing our lives together. Our love was genuine and planned by God; otherwise "Doni and Dani" would have never happened. My prayer now is that everyone involved will learn the value of God's love in our hearts which is the very center of all our journeys acquired in our lifetimes.

FORGIVENESS

God's love and mercy heals our heart
And helps us find our way
Our faith in Him is all we need
When facing each new day.

Forgiveness comes from deep within
A gift from God above
Happiness rewards our lives
When sharing in God's love.

Time will change the hurt you feel
And life begins anew
Thank God for blessings he bestows
In everything you do.

75916225R00091

Made in the USA
Columbia, SC
28 August 2017